Arthur Abraham

Undefeated IBF Middleweight Champion of the World

10.12.2005 - 10.07.2009

Seine Welt ist der Sport - Ulli Wegner

Kurz: 26.04.1942 in Stettin geboren; in Penkun Mecklenburg-Vorpommern aufgewachsen; hat Traktoren- und Landmaschinenschlosser gelernt; bei der Marine gedient; im Bergbau gearbeitet; und immer geboxt! Als Amateurtrainer erzielte er mit seinen Aktiven zahlreiche internationale Erfolge und als Profitrainer hat er eine Weltmeisterschaftsschmiede aufgebaut (Sven Ottke, Markus Beyer, Marco Huck, Arthur Abraham und Cecilia Breakhus). King Arthur mit seinem enormen Willen, sich einen Platz in der Weltspitze zu sichern, gehört wohl zu seinen spektakulärsten Schützlingen. In feinster Filigranarbeit wurden Rohdiamanten zu Brillanten geschliffen, ein glasharter Weg mit täglich neuen Herausforderungen. Jeder seiner Boxer braucht seine eigene, immer neue Motivation zur Höchstleistung. Seine raue Stimme in der Ringecke hören seine Jungs – „Pardon, auch seine Firstlady": „Komm mein Junge, das machst Du richtig, das kannst Du!" Oder auch mal: „Boxe jetzt endlich, hau ihn weg!" An jedem Boxabend knistert die Luft in der Arena vor Spannung, Erfolgserwartung und Siegeswille. Die Gesichter der Zuschauer zeigen Emotionen, denn alle spüren bei den Akteuren im Ring die Anspannung, die große Achtung, den gesunden Respekt und ganz viel Vertrauen zu Ihrem Trainer. Oder eben für Arthur „ein Indianer kennt keinen Schmerz!"

Sport is his world - Ulli Wegner

Briefly: Born in Stettin on 26.04.1942; Grew up in Penkun, Mecklenburg-Vorpommern; trained to be a tractor and agricultural machinery mechanic; served in the Marines; worked down the mine; and has always boxed! He picked up numerous international successes with his pupils during his amateur coaching career and, as a professional coach, he has expanded his crew of World Champions (which now includes Sven Ottke, Markus Beyer, Marco Huck, Arthur Abraham and Cecilia Braekhus). King Arthur, with his determination to take his place on top of the world, is surely one of his most spectacular protégés. Working meticulously, he has ground raw diamonds into jewels, following a clearly defined process with fresh, new challenges every day. Each of his boxers needs their own, constantly evolving motivation to perform to their highest level. His boys - sorry, also his First Lady - hear his hoarse voice from the corner of the ring: "Come on my boy, that's right, you can do it!" or sometimes: "Start boxing, knock him out!" Tension, expectations and the will to win fill the air in the arena on boxing nights. The spectators' faces display their own emotions since everybody can feel the tension of the protagonists inside the ring and their great attention, their healthy respect and a lot of faith in their coach. Or in Arthur's case: "An Indian knows no pain!"

Nächste Seite: Das Fachmagazin "BoxSport" wählte Arthur Abraham und Ulli Wegner 2010 zu "Boxer und Trainer des Jahres"

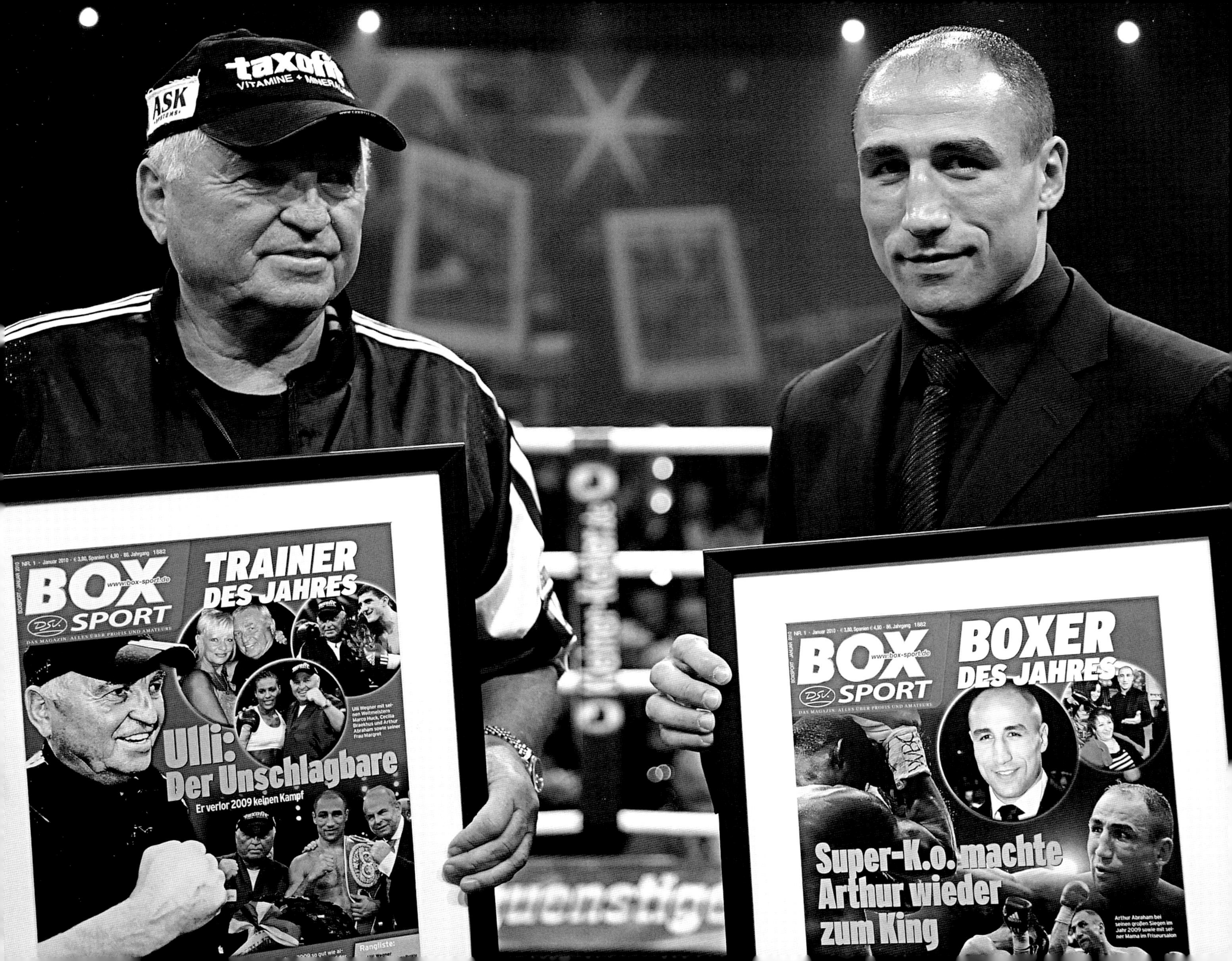
taxofit
VITAMINE
ASK
NR. 1 · Januar 2010 · € 3,80, Spanien € 4,90 · 86. Jahrgang 1682
BOX
www.box-sport.de
SPORT
DAS MAGAZIN. ALLES ÜBER PROFIS UND AMATEURE
TRAINER DES JAHRES
Ulli Wegner mit seinen Weltmeistern Marco Huck, Cecilia Braekhus und Arthur Abraham sowie seiner Frau Margret
Ulli: Der Unschlagbare
Er verlor 2009 keinen Kampf
Rangliste:
NR. 1 · Januar 2010 · € 3,80, Spanien € 4,90 · 86. Jahrgang 1682
BOX
www.box-sport.de
SPORT
DAS MAGAZIN. ALLES ÜBER PROFIS UND AMATEURE
BOXER DES JAHRES
Super-K.o. machte Arthur wieder zum King
Arthur Abraham bei seinen großen Siegen im Jahr 2009 sowie mit seiner Mama im Friseursalon

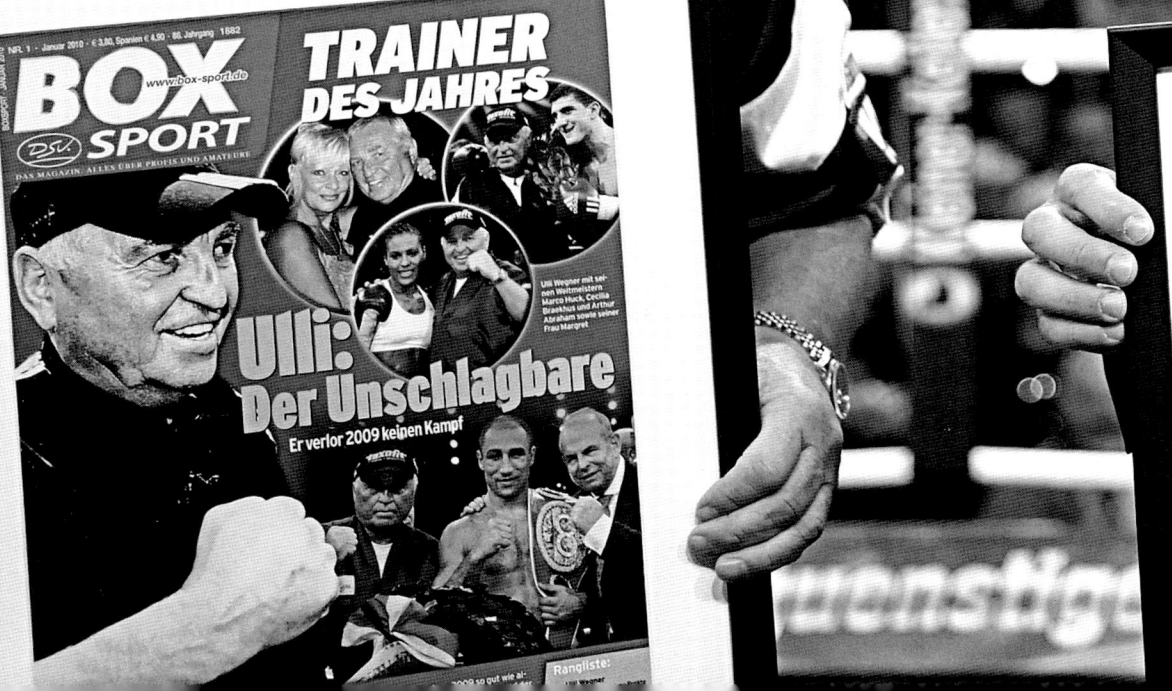

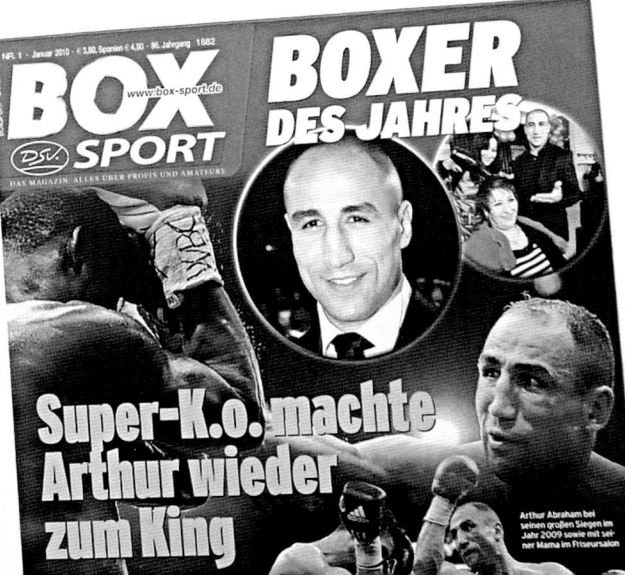

Arthur Abraham vom Schlumpfboxer zum KING ARTHUR

Arthur Abraham wurde als Avetik Abrahamyan am 20. Februar 1980 in Eriwan, Armenien geboren. Nach 90 Kämpfen als Amateur begann er am 16. August 2003 seine Laufbahn als Profiboxer. Ein für ihn sicherlich unvergessliches Datum in seiner Laufbahn war der 10.12.2005 als er gegen Kingsley IKEKE in Leipzig den Weltmeistertitel des IBF im Mittelgewicht gewann. Arthur Abraham kämpfte bis zur „Blutschlacht von Wetzlar" als der Schlumpfboxer. Dies gefiel ihm zwar nicht sonderlich aber es war sehr werbewirksam. Aus urheberrechtlichen Gründen durfte er dann nicht mehr zu dem Lied von Vadder Abraham einmarschieren und war fortan KING ARTHUR, was auch den Tatsachen entspricht. Von 30 Kämpfen im Mittelgewicht gewann Abraham 25 durch K.o. Als Weltmeister verteidigte er 10-mal erfolgreich seinen Titel. Der Rückkampf gegen Miranda in Florida fand außerhalb des Mittelgewichts statt, so dass nur 29 Kämpfe mit 24 K.o.'s im Mittelgewicht stattfanden. Der Wunsch als Superchamp das Mittelgewicht verlassen zu können wurde durch die Verweigerung zum Kampf von Kelly PAVLIK und Felix STURM zunichte gemacht. Da er keine Gegner mehr fand gab ABRAHAM am 10. Juli 2009 seinen Gürtel zurück und wechselte ins SUPERMITTELGEWICHT. Arthur Abraham hat seit 2006 die deutsche Staatsbürgerschaft. Während seiner Zeit als IBF Weltmeister war er neben Ulli Wegner Hauptakteur in der Boxsportdokumentation, „ES GEHT UM ALLES" sowie Schauspieler in dem Film, „MAX SCHMELING" mit Henry Maske in der Hauptrolle.

Arthur Abraham - from a Smurf boxer to KING ARTHUR

Arthur Abraham was born as Avetik Abrahamyan on February 20, 1980 in Eriwan, Armenia. After 90 amateur fights, he began his career as a professional boxer on August 16, 2003. A date he will certainly never forget is December 10, 2005, when he won the World Title in the IBF Middleweight division by beating Kingsley IKEKE in Leipzig. Arthur Abraham fought as the 'Smurf boxer', until his "bloody slaughter in Wetzlar". He may not have liked this all that much, but it was very effective publicity. Due to copyright laws, however, he was no longer able to walk out to the Vadder Abraham song, and from then on, he became known as KING ARTHUR - a worthy name. In 30 Middleweight fights, Abraham won 30 with 25 by K.O, and he defended his world title 10 times. His rematch with Miranda in Florida was not actually in the Middleweight division, so only 29 fights with 24 K.Os actually took place as a Middleweight. He was denied his desire to leave Middleweight as the Superchamp when Kelly PAVLIK and Felix STURM both turned down fights. Since he could not find any other opponent, ABRAHAM gave his belt back on July 10, 2009, and switched into the Super-Middleweight division. Arthur Abraham has German citizenship since 2006. During his time as IBF World Champion, he was the main protagonist in the boxing documentary "ES GEHT UM ALLES" ('Everything is at stake') along with Ulli Wegner, and he was also an actor in the film "MAX SCHMELLING" with Henry Maske playing the lead role.

DIE FOTOGRAFIN MARIANNE MÜLLER

Marianne Müller wurde 1953 in Bochum geboren. Ihre Eltern waren beide Sportfotografen. Diese Leidenschaft übertrug sich auch auf sie. Ihre ersten Sportfotos schoss sie schon mit 14 Jahren. Eine Lehre mit den Volontären im elterlichen Betrieb vermittelte noch weiteres praktisches und theoretisches Wissen zu dem bereits vorhandenen Können. Ein Französischstudium sowie das Studium der Sozialpädagogik rundeten die Ausbildung ab. Nach ca. 10 Jahren in der Arbeits- und Obdachlosenhilfe zog es sie zurück zur alten Leidenschaft: der Sportfotografie. Vorwiegend wurde American Football aber auch Fußball und Eishockey fotografiert. Die Handballfotografie ist trotz der hauptsächlichen Boxsportfotografie, seit 1992, immer noch ihre Passion.

THE PHOTOGRAPHER MARIANNE MÜLLER

Marianne Müller was born in Bochum in 1953. Her parents were both sports photographers and they passed down this passion to her. She took her first sports photographs at the age of 14 and an apprenticeship in her parents' company gave her even more practical and theoretical knowledge to go with her natural ability. A course in French and the study of Social Pedagogy rounded off her education. After approximately 10 years assisting the unemployed and the homeless, she returned to her passion of sports photography. She mainly photographed American football, but also football and ice hockey. Handball photography remains her passion, despite focusing mainly on boxing photography since 1992.

FOTOGRAF WERNER DITTMAIR

Born: 22. 07. 1948 and still alive!
Durch die professionelle journalistische Boxsportfotografie sowie Fotografie von Musikern und Stars wird die Passion des Fotografierens befriedigt. Einer autodidaktischen Fortbildung mittels Lehrbüchern des Großmeisters der Fotografie, Ansel Adams, sowie den hervorragenden Fachbüchern von Jost J. Marchesi und internationaler Fachliteratur folgte eine Ausbildung an der Akademie der Bayerischen Presse in München, Bereich Fotografie. Weitere Seminare an dem Institut für konzeptionelle Fotografie in Duisburg folgten. Durch die Teilnahme an sämtlichen Seminaren von Andreas Weidner, Deutschlands wohl bekanntestem Lehrmeister der schwarz-weiss Fotografie und Meister aller Grautöne sowie Herausgeber von hervorragenden Lehrbüchern, Publikationen und internationalen Bildausstellungen, wurde die Fotolaborarbeit par excellence vermittelt. Durch den persönlichen Kontakt mit vielen Boxern sowie Stars von Bühne und Fernsehen wurden viele einzigartige Bilder ermöglicht. Auch das alte Handwerk des Barytprints wird beherrscht und angewandt.

THE PHOTOGRAPHER WERNER DITTMAIR

Born: 22.07.1948 and still alive!
His passion for photography is satisfied with his professional journalistic boxing photography as well as by photographing musicians and celebrities. Following an education at the Akademie der Bayerischen Presse (Bavarian Press Academy), photography division, in Munich, he has continued his education by himself using the educational publications of the great photographic master Ansel Adams, as well as several excellent handbooks by Jost J. Marchesi and other international educational literature. Further seminars at the Institut für konzeptionelle Fotografie in Duisburg followed. Participation in numerous seminars of Andreas Weidner, probably Germany's most famous master in black and white photography and the master of grey toning, as well as the author of excellent guidebooks, publications and international photo exhibitions, provided the ultimate lesson in photographic laboratory work. As a freelance photographer, his already large portfolio is constantly expanding. Personal contacts with many boxers as well as stars of stage and screen have made unique pictures possible. The old technique of Baryt-print is also being mastered and employed.

Arthur Abraham vs Kingsley Ikeke
Vacant IBF middleweight title
10.12.2005 Leipziger Arena
Leipzig, Deutschland
Fotos: Marianne Müller

Der 10. 12. 2005 wird wahrscheinlich ein unvergessliches Datum in Arthur Abrahams Leben bleiben. Als IBF Weltmeister im Mittelgewicht verließ er, vor Freude weinend, den Ring im Kampf gegen den als sehr stark geltenden Kingsley IKEKE. Ein spektakulärer K.o. in der 5. Runde begrub die Träume des Nigerianes als Sieger den Ring zu verlassen. In einem fantastischen Kampf führte jedoch Arthur Abraham in allen Runden.

December 12, 2005, will probably be an unforgettable date in the life of Arthur Abraham. He left the ring crying with joy as the new IBF World Champion in Middleweight after his fight with the highly-rated Kingsley IKEKE. A spectacular knockout in the fifth round ended the Nigerian's dreams of leaving the ring triumphant. Arthur Abraham led on points in every single round of a fantastic fight.

Arthur Abraham und Bruder Alexander

Hako Sevecke, Ulli Wegner, Arthur Abraham, Wilfried Sauerland und Alexander Abraham

Lothar Kannenberg und Weltmeister Arthur Abraham

Arthur Abraham vs Shannan Taylor
IBF middleweight title
04.03.2006 EWE-Arena
Oldenburg, Deutschland
Fotos: Marianne Müller

Seine erste Titelverteidigung gewann ABRAHAM durch einen Punktsieg.
Der Kampf ging über die volle Distanz von 12 Runden.

ABRAHAM won his first title defence on a points' decision.
The fight went the entire 12-rounds' distance.

Hagen Döring, Arthur Abraham, Ulli Wegner und Hako Sevecke

Arthur Abraham vs Kofi Jantuah
IBF middleweight title
13.05.2006 Stadthalle
Zwickau, Deutschland
Fotos: Marianne Müller

Auch nach 12 Runden wilden Schlaghagels und harten Treffern an den Kopf des Herausforderers aus Ghana vermochten diesen nicht zu Boden zu bringen. Der mit einem wahrhaftigen Eisenschädel versehene Jantuah wußte sich aber auch zu wehren und landete selbst so manchen Treffer. Ein hohes Tempo, ein starker Kampf und ein nicht K.o. zu schlagender Gegner ist die Bilanz dieser 2. Titelverteidigung, welche mit einem Punktsieg für Arthur Abraham endete.

Even after 12 rounds of wild blows and strong strikes to the head, his challenger from Ghana still did not want to go to ground. Jantuah, whose head must have been made of steel, also knew how to defend himself and he also landed several punches of his own. It was a high-tempo, strong fight and this second title defence did not end in a knockout, but Arthur Abraham still triumphed on points.

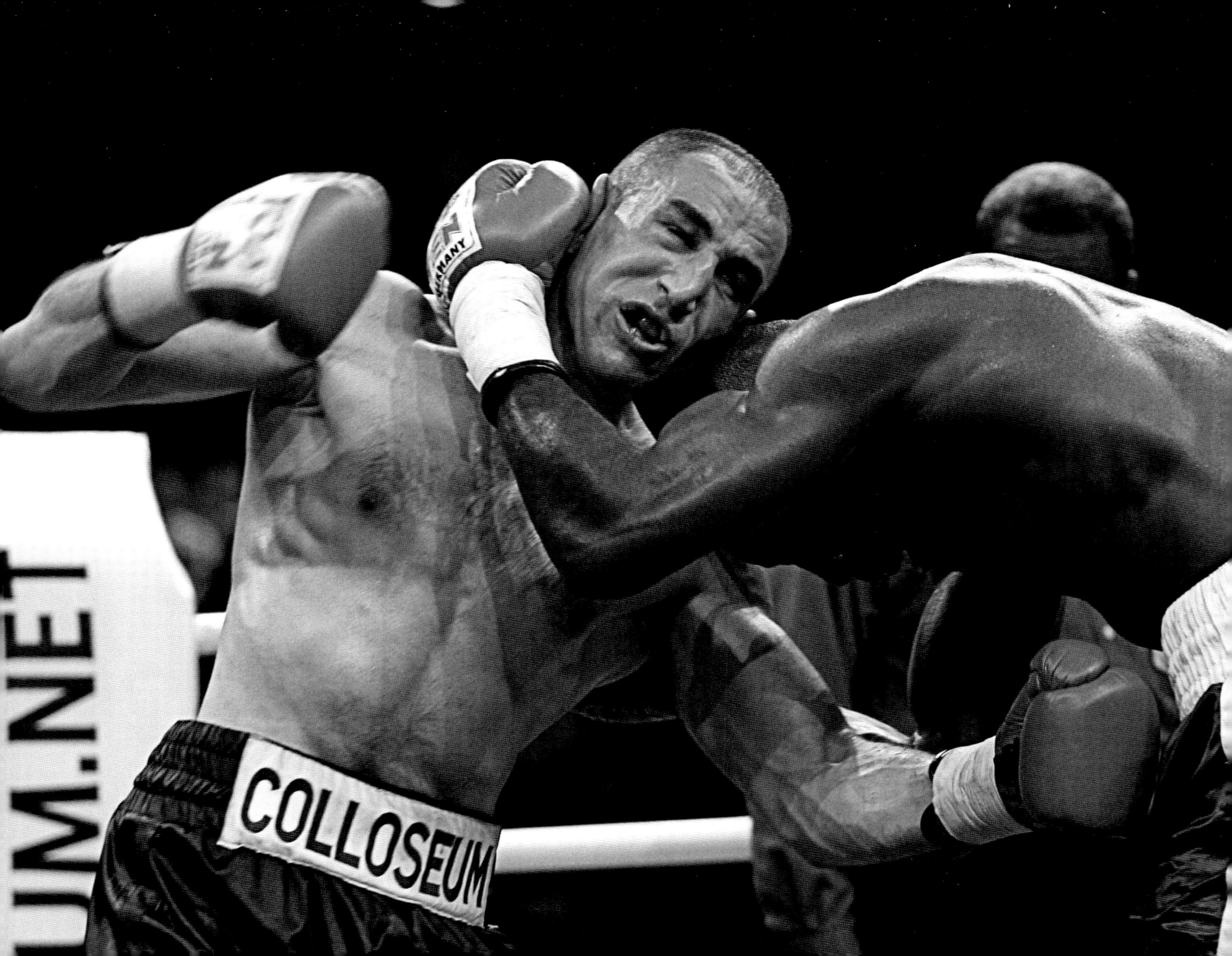

Arthur Abraham vs Edison Miranda
IBF middleweight title
23.09.2006 Rittal Arena
Wetzlar, Deutschland
Fotos: Marianne Müller

Ein Boxkampf der Geschichte schrieb und unvergesslich bleibt: Ob der Kopfstoß von Miranda in der 5. Runde oder eine Schlagwirkung in der 4. Runde den Kiefer von King Arthur in der Rittal Arena von Wetzlar gleich doppelt brach, wird ungeklärt bleiben. Am Ende verteidigte Abraham seinen Titel in einer grandiosen Ringschlacht blutüberströmt mit gebrochenem Kiefer. Der Champion begann stark. In der Behandlungspause nach dem Kopfstoß diagnostizierte Ringarzt Professor Walter Wagner den Kieferbruch. Der Ringrichter wollte den Kampf zu Gunsten des Titelverteidigers abbrechen, doch der IBF-Supervisor sah den Kopfstoß nicht als ausschlaggebend für die Verletzung. Also kämpfte der IBF-Champion weiter und wuchs über sich hinaus. Der stürmisch und unsauber boxende Miranda erhielt aufgrund von Tiefschlägen in der 7. und 11. Runde weitere Punktabzüge. Abraham revanchierte sich auf sportliche Art und Weise - mit sehr harten Treffern. Am Ende gewann er diese Schlacht einstimmig nach Punkten. Der bis dahin ungeschlagene Kolumbianer Miranda sollte aber noch eine eindeutigere Box-Lehrstunde im Rückkampf in Amerika bekommen.

A fight which wrote history and will remain unforgettable: Whether it was Miranda's headbutt in the fifrth round or the after-effects of a punch in the fourth round which broke King Arthurs jaw in two places in the Rittal Arena in Wetzlar remains a mystery. In the end, Abraham, covered in blood and with a broken jaw, defended his title in a magnificent slaughter in the ring. The champion started strongly. During the pause for treatment after the headbutt, ring doctor Professor Walter Wagner diagnosed the broken jaw. The referee wanted to end the fight and award it to the defending champion, but the IBF supervisor did not view the headbutt as the cause of the injury. So the IBF champion fought on, and he exceeded himself. The stormy and dirty boxing Miranda was deducted further points in the seventh and 11th rounds due to low blows and Abraham gained his revenge in a sporting way with very hard punches. In the end, he won the slaughter with a unanimous points' victory. The previously unbeaten Miranda was to be given an even clearer boxing lesson in the rematch in America.

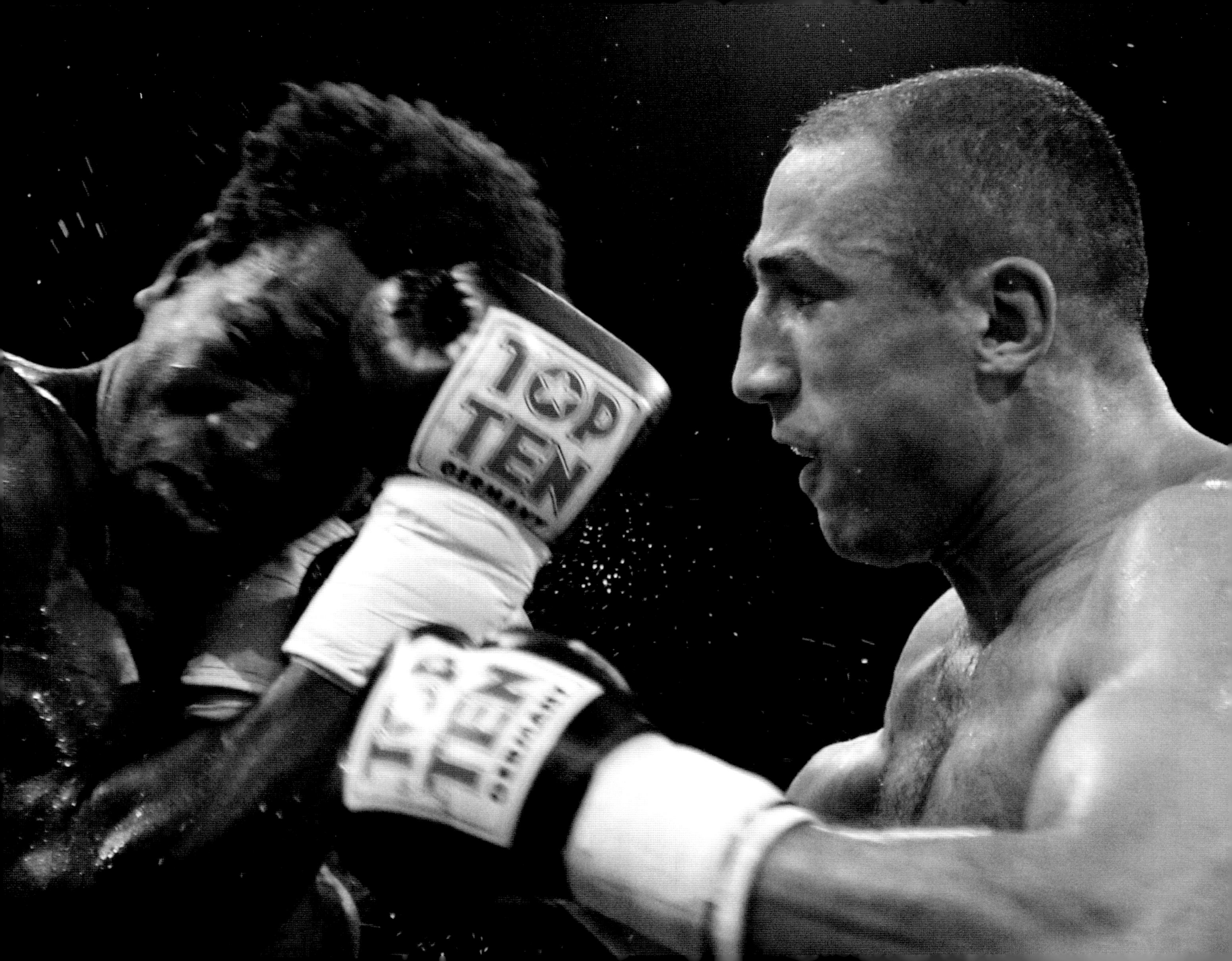
TOP TEN
TOP TEN

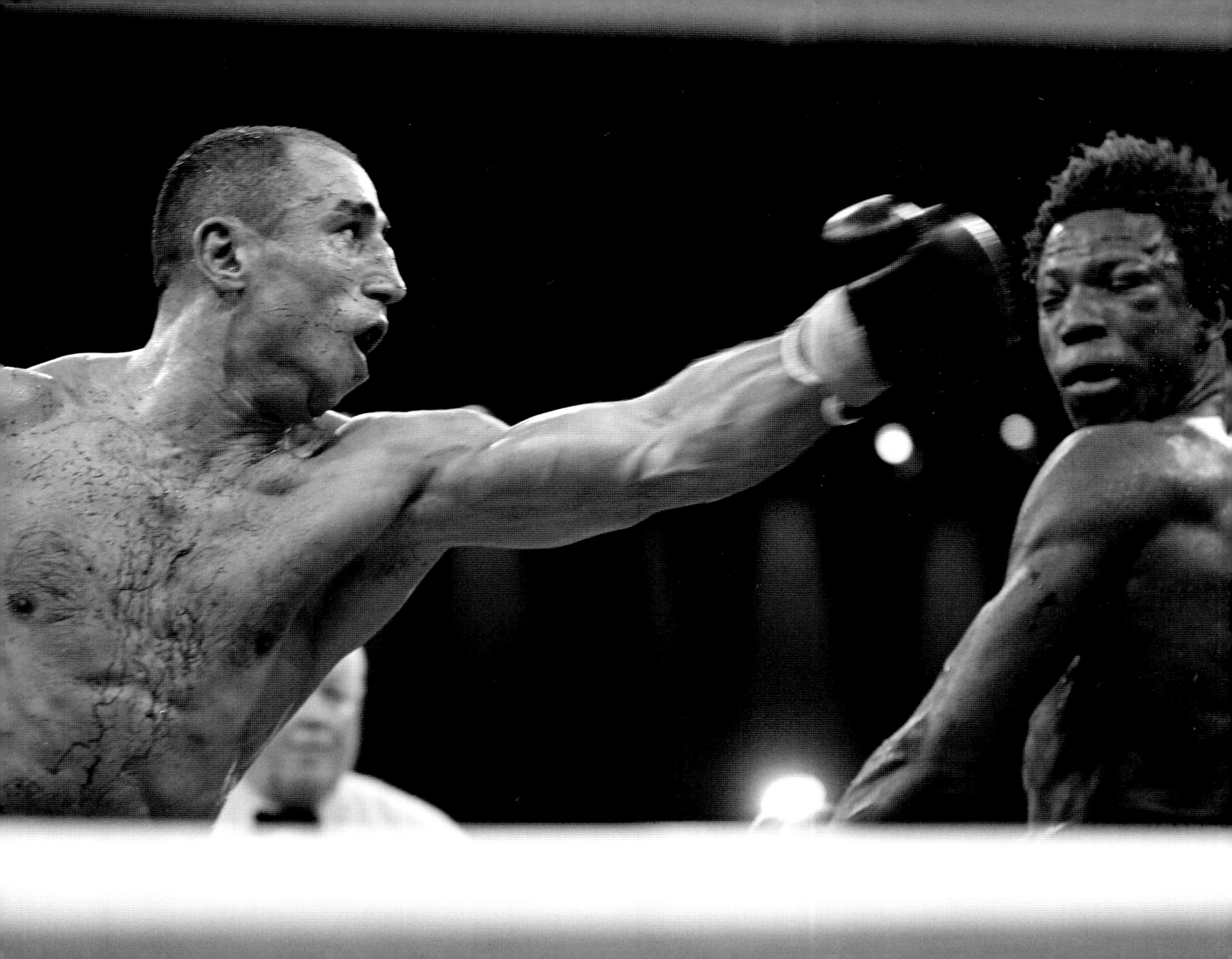

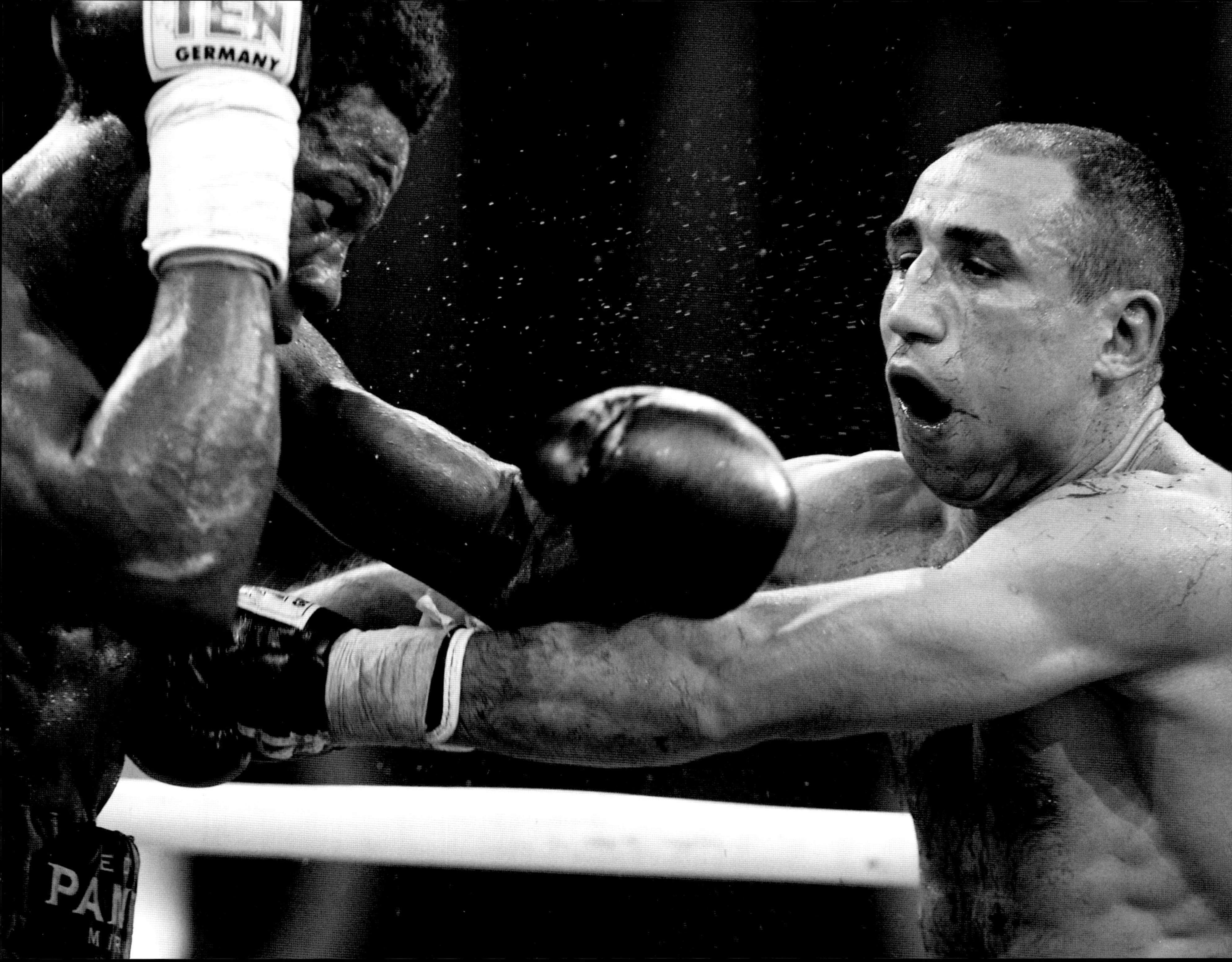
GERMANY

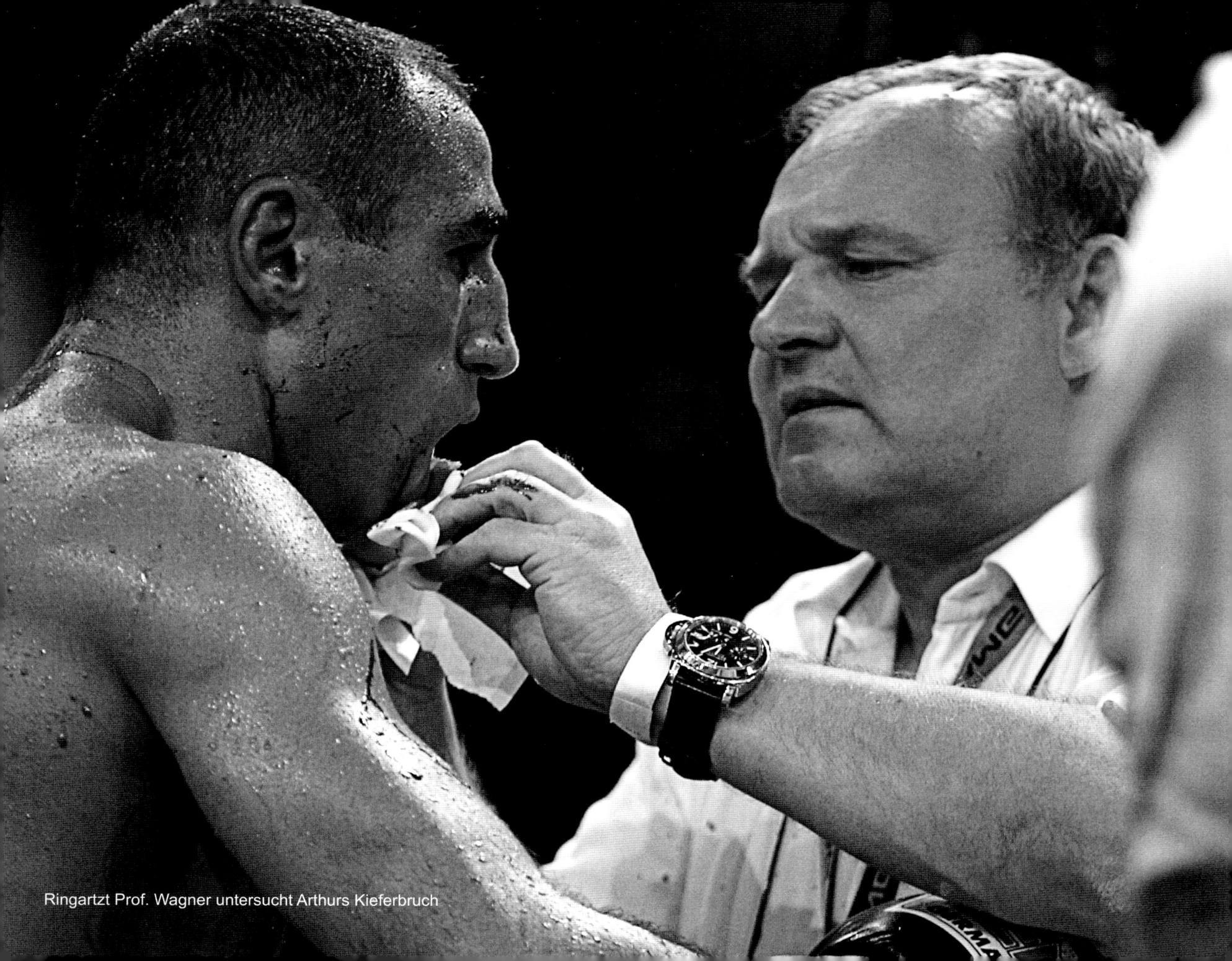

Ringartzt Prof. Wagner untersucht Arthurs Kieferbruch

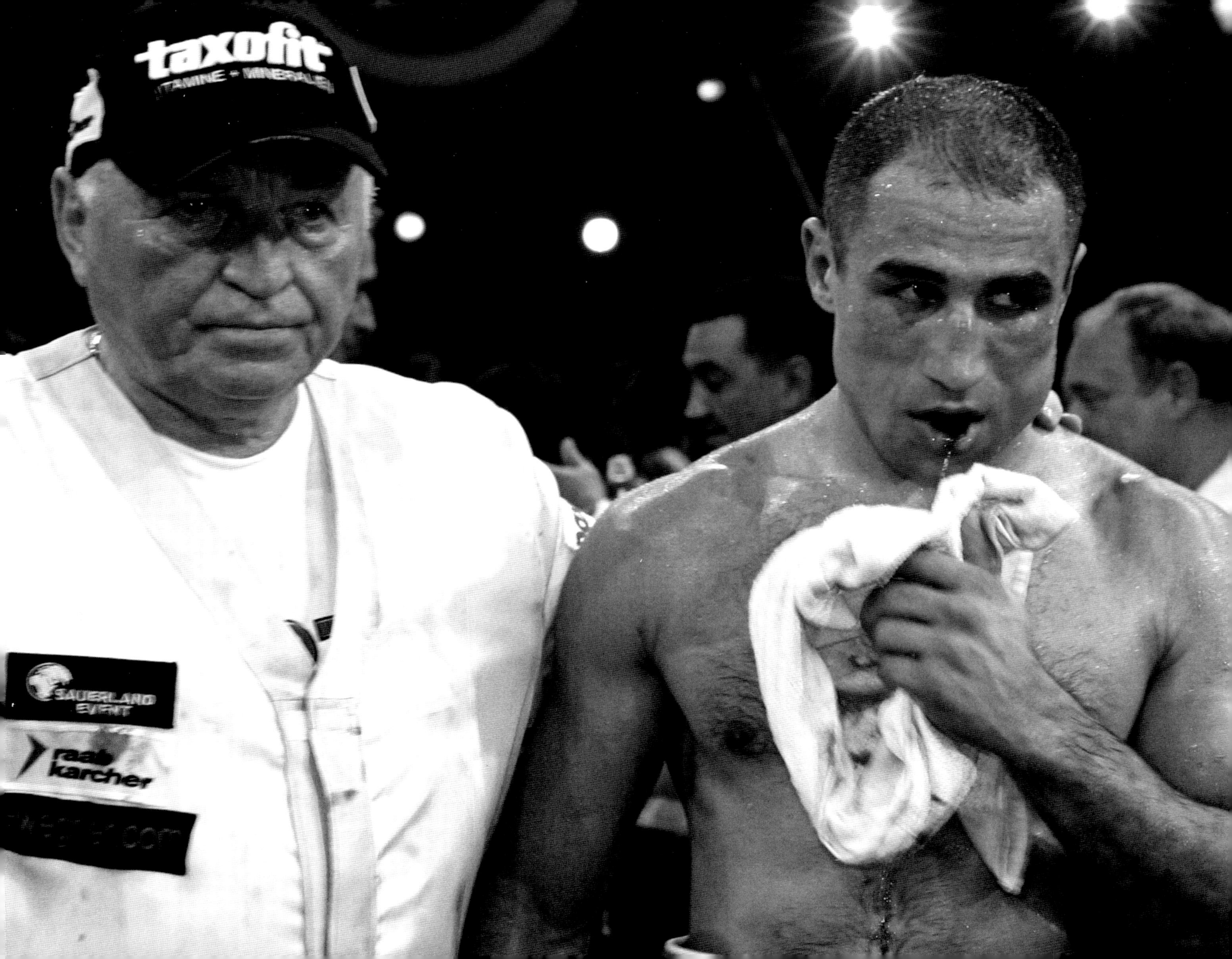
taxofit
SAUERLAND
raab karcher

Arthur Abraham vs Sebastien Demers
IBF middleweight title
26.05.2007 Jako-Arena
Bamberg, Deutschland
Fotos: Werner Dittmair

Die erste Titelverteidigung nach der Blut-Schlacht von Wetzlar war zugleich die kürzeste Titelverteidigung in seiner Karriere als Weltmeister. Nach achtmonatiger Regenerationspause bekam Demers in der dritten Runde sehr eindringlich seine Grenzen aufgezeigt und wurde durch einen K.o. von seinem Wunschdenken neuer Weltmeister zu werden, befreit.

The first title defence after the bloody slaughter in Wetzlar was also the shortest title defence in his career as World Champion. After an eight-month spell of recuperation, Demers was given his clear comeuppance in the third round and his dreams of becoming World Champion were erased with a knockout.

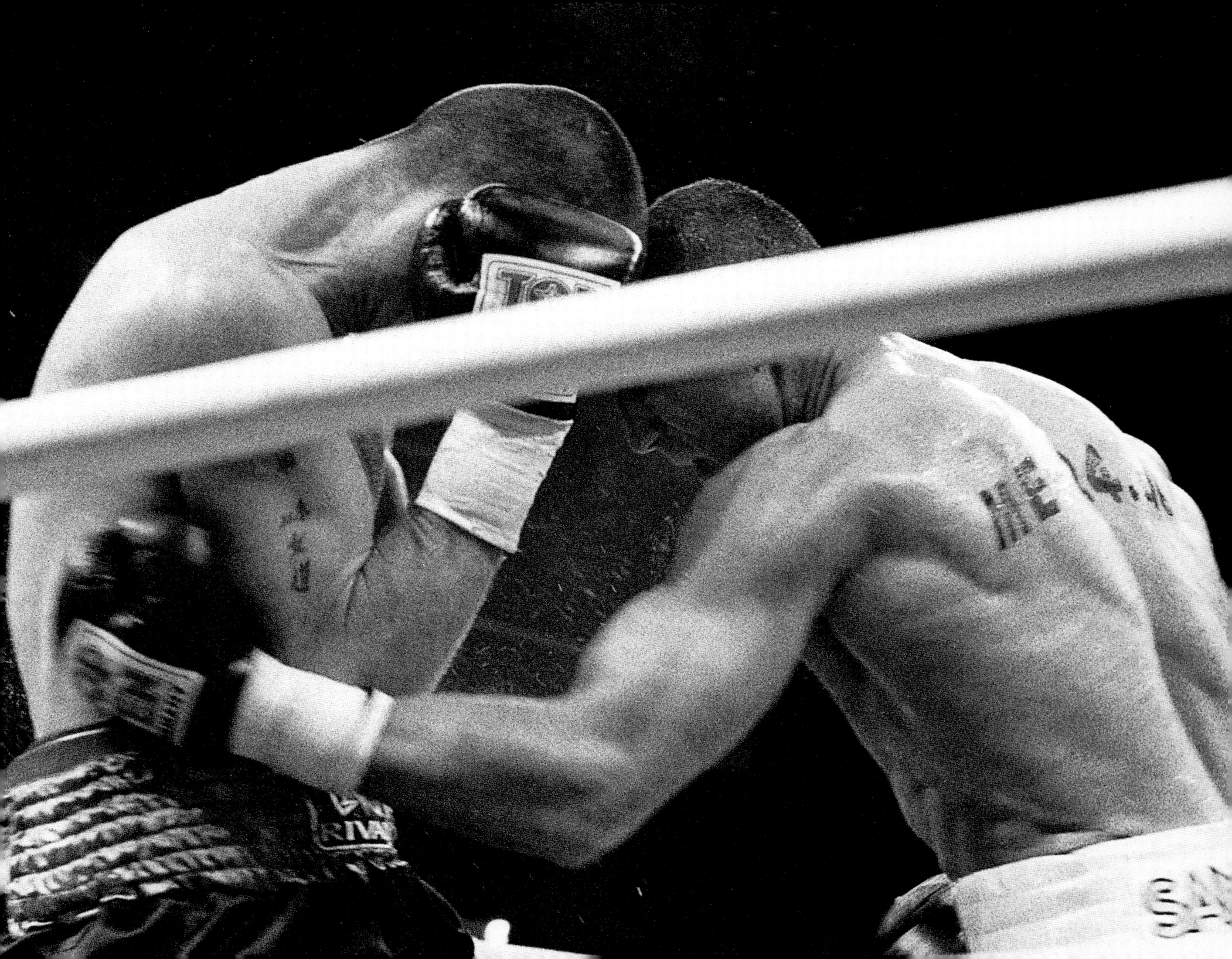
RIVA

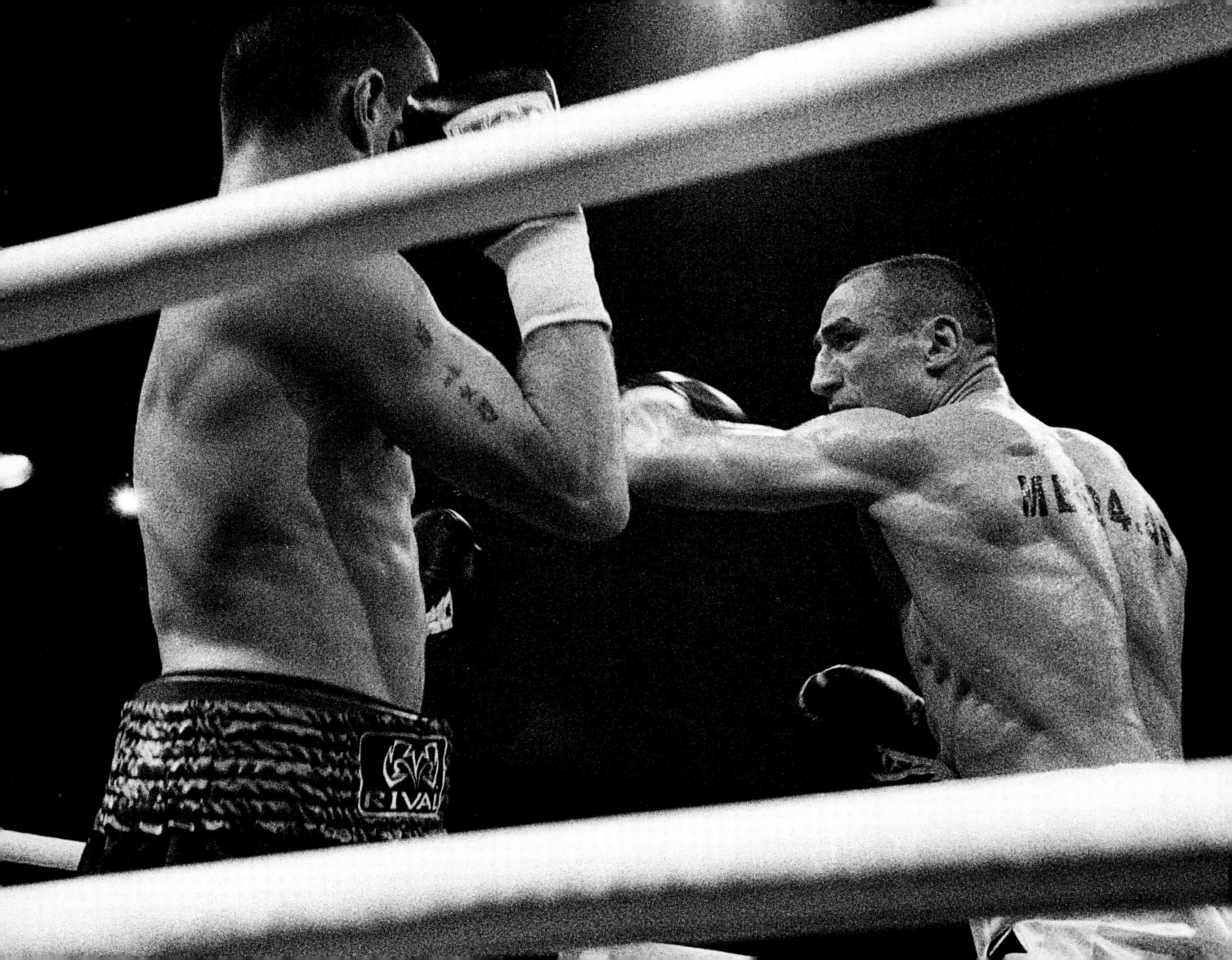
RIVAL

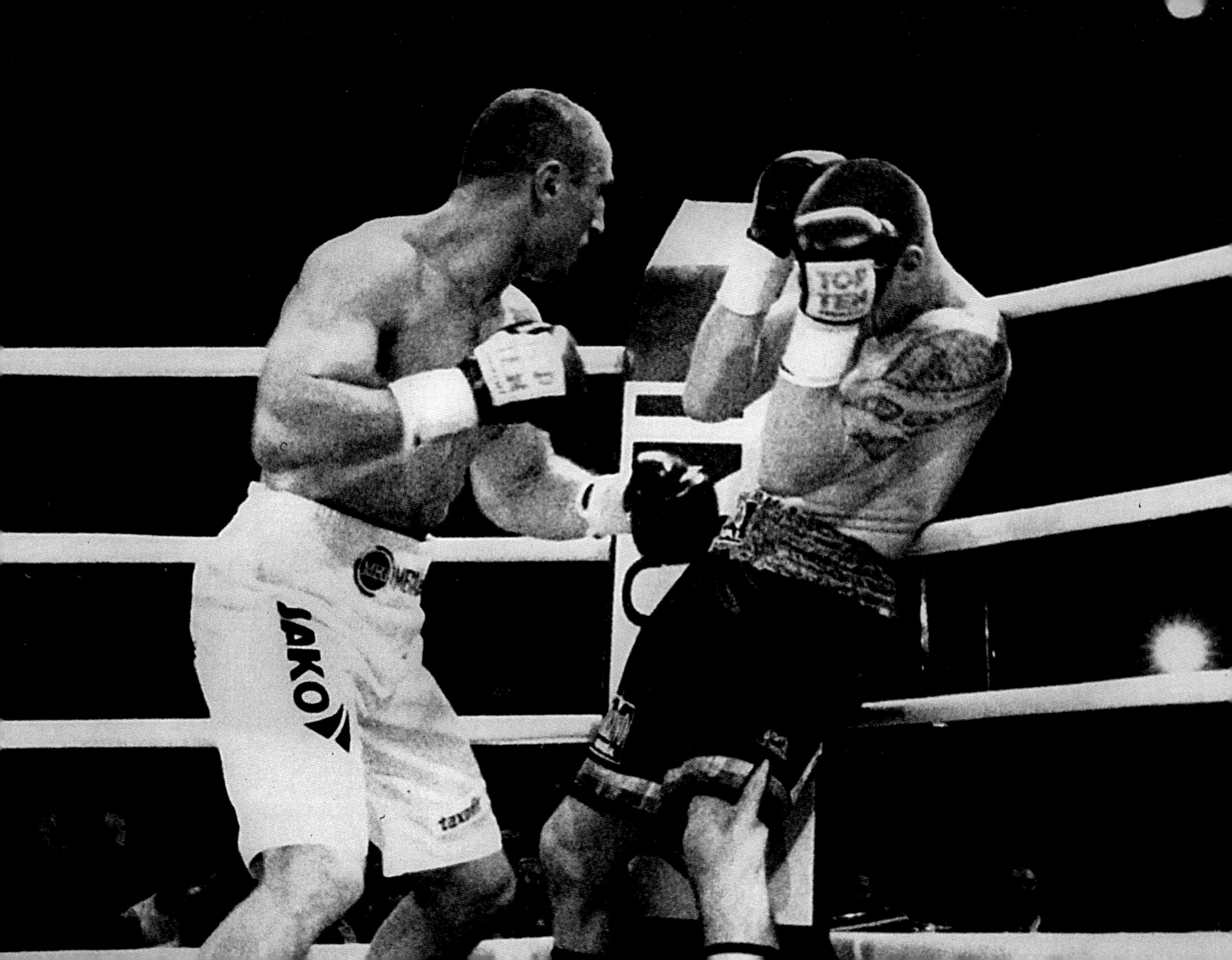
JAKO
TOP TEN

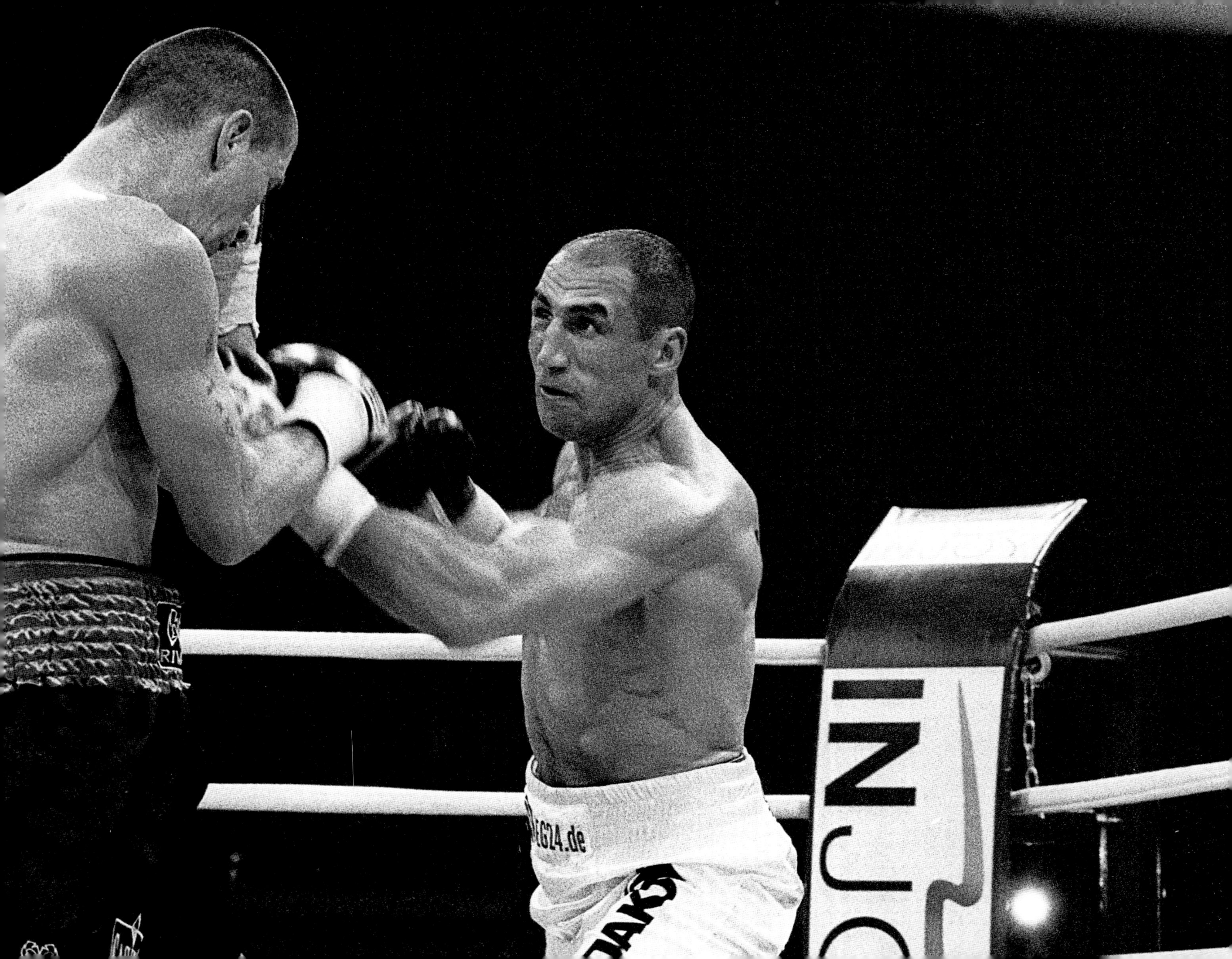

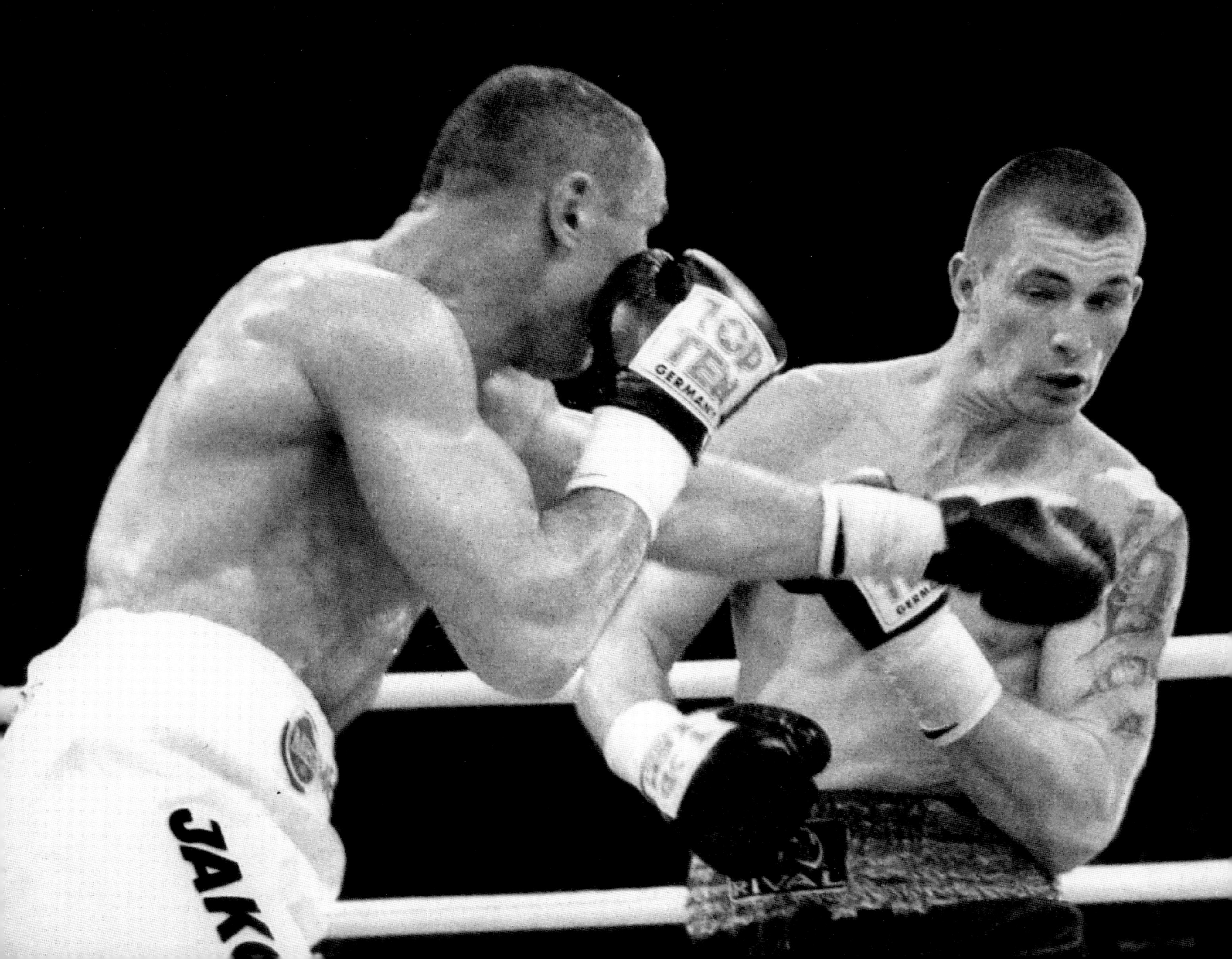
RIVAL

Arthur Abraham vs Khoren Gevor
IBF middleweight title
18.08.2007 Max Schmeling Halle
Berlin, Deutschland
Fotos: Werner Dittmair

"Mehr K.o. geht nicht" schrieb die BILD Zeitung über den Niederschlag seines armenischen Landmanns 19 Sekunden vor Ende der 11. Runde. Der linke Aufwärtshaken von King Arthur hatte eine minutenlange Bewusstlosigkeit zur Folge und Gevor verließ am nächsten Tag das Krankenhaus mit einer schweren Gehirnerschütterung. Die hervorragenden Nehmerqualitäten von Gevor verhinderten einen früheren K.o. durch King Arthur in dessen 5. Titelverteidigung.

'There is nothing more knockout than this' titled the Bild newspaper after the defeat of his Armenian compatriot 19 seconds before the end of the 11th round. The left-handed upper cuts from King Arthur left Gevor unconscious for a minute and he only left hospital the next day with severe concussion. The excellent resistance qualities of Gevor prevented him from an earlier knockout as King Arthur completed his fifth title defence.

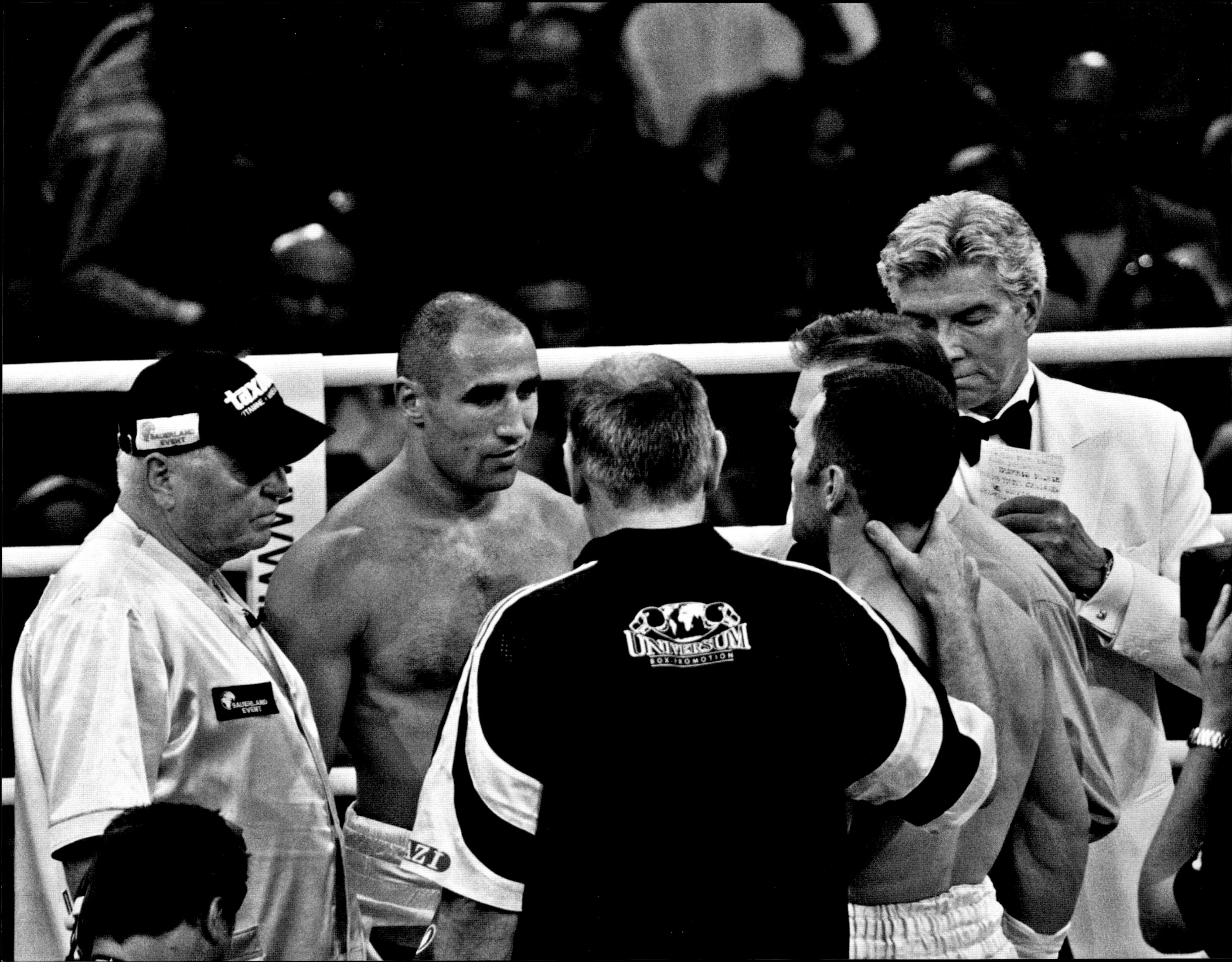
SAUERLAND EVENT
UNIVERSUM
BOX-PROMOTION
SAUERLAND EVENT

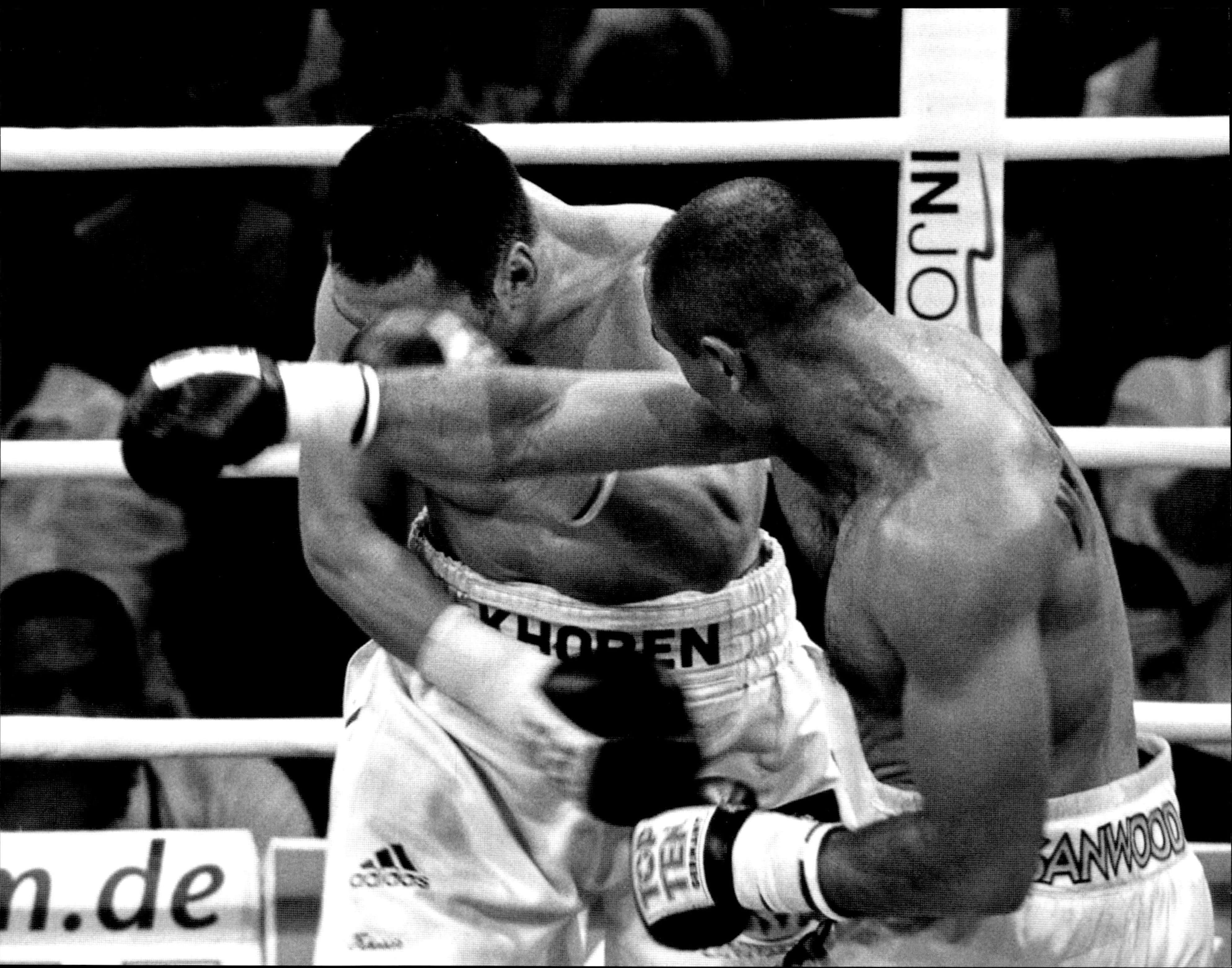
KHOREN
m.de
adidas

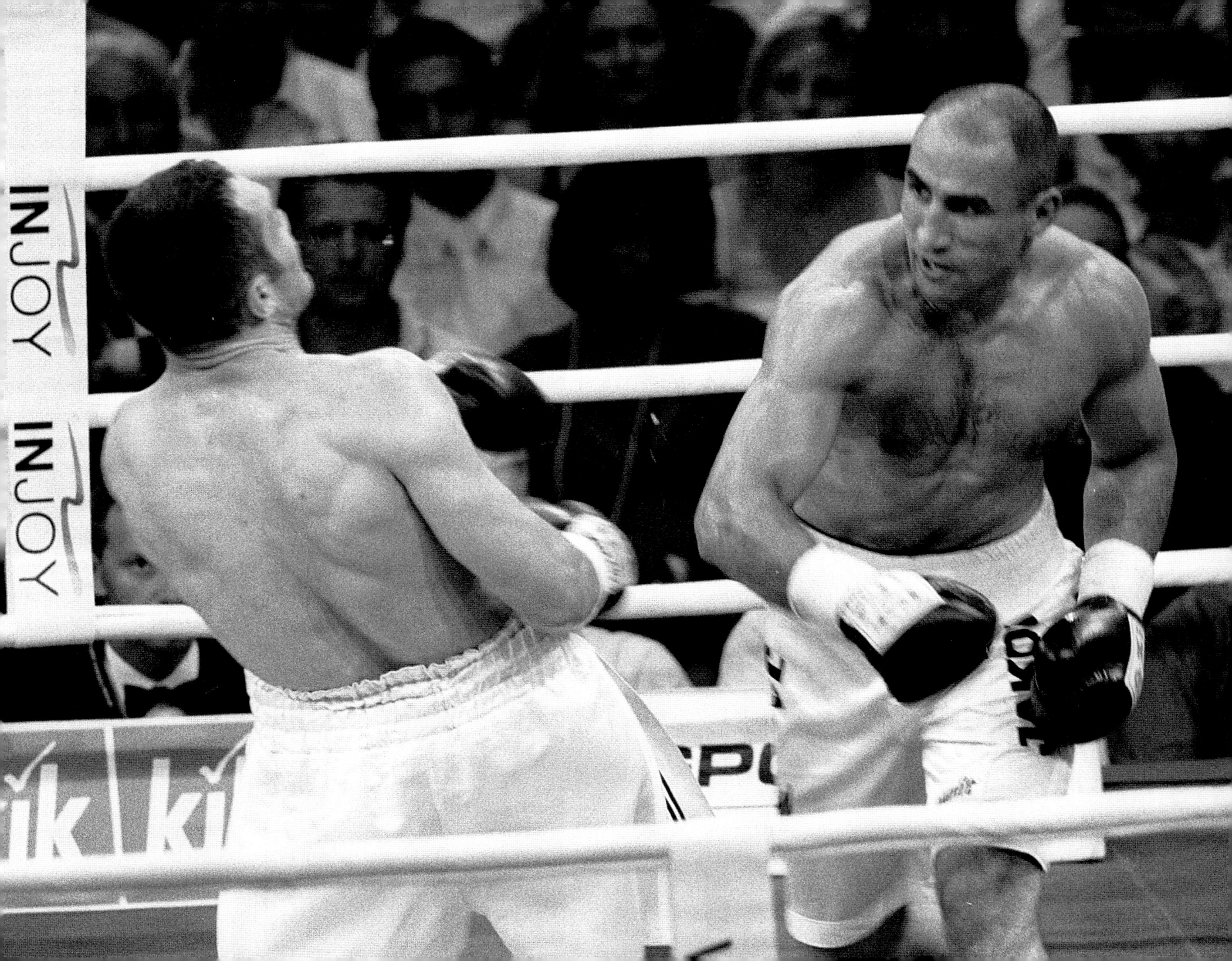
INJOY
INJOY

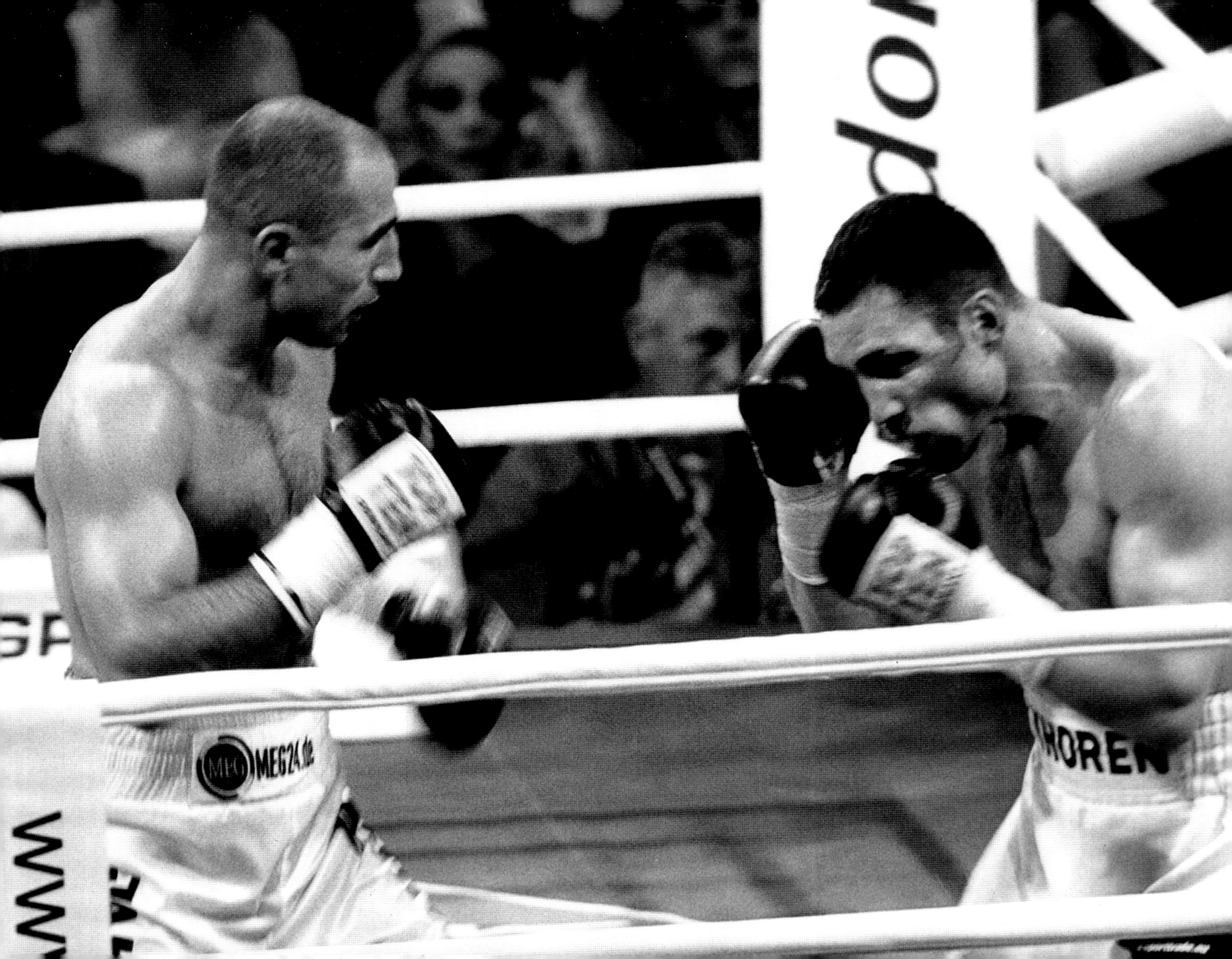
MEG24.de

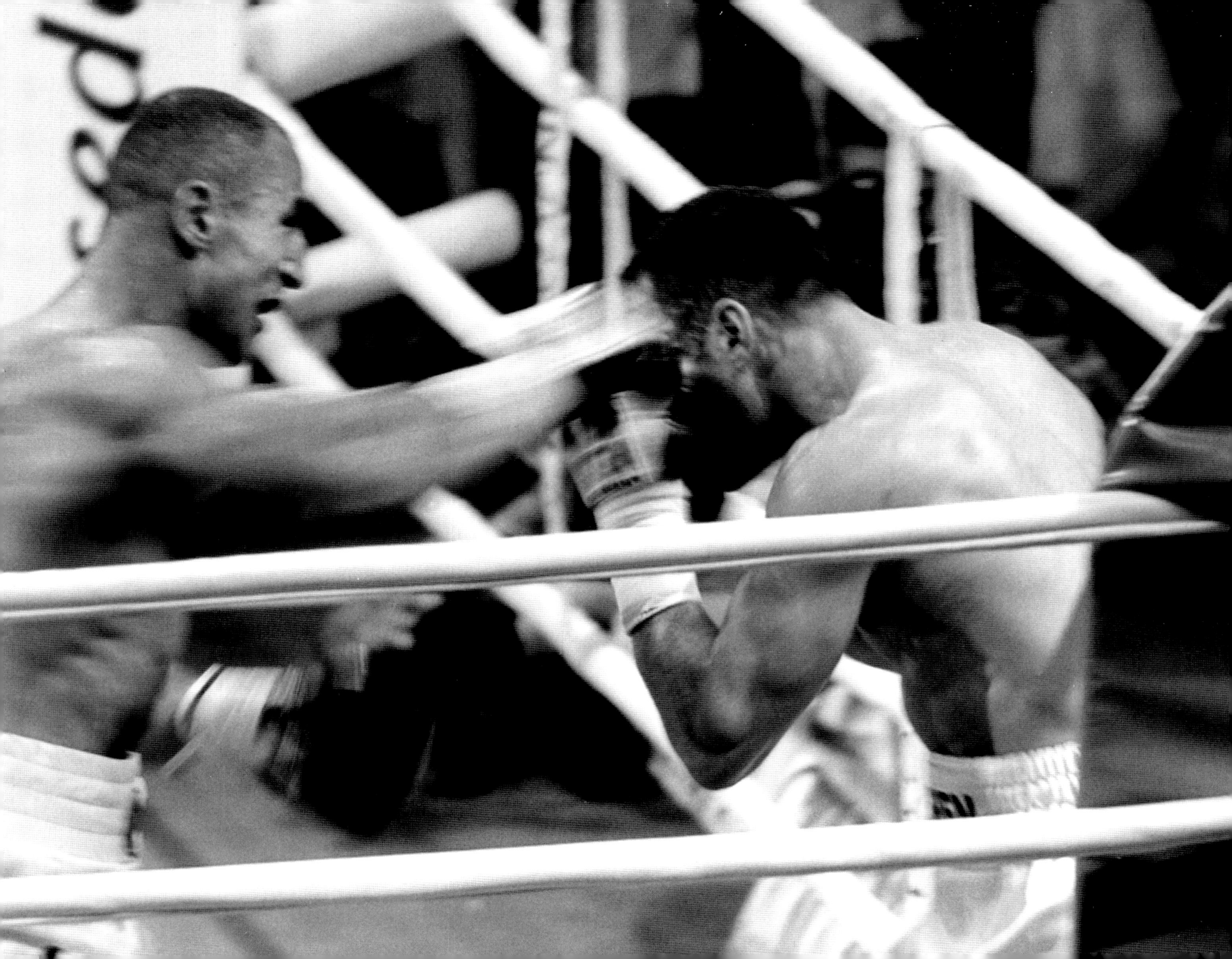

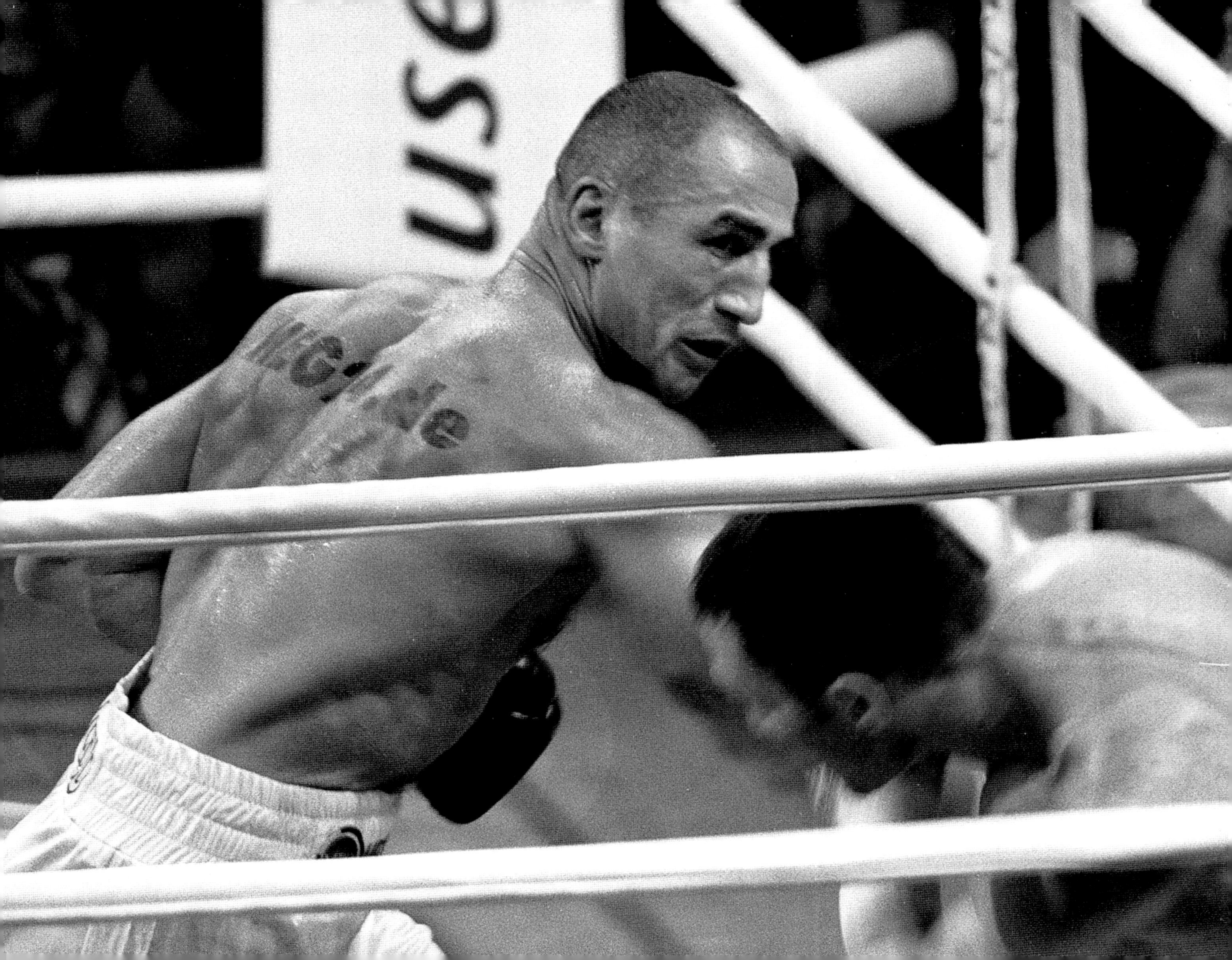

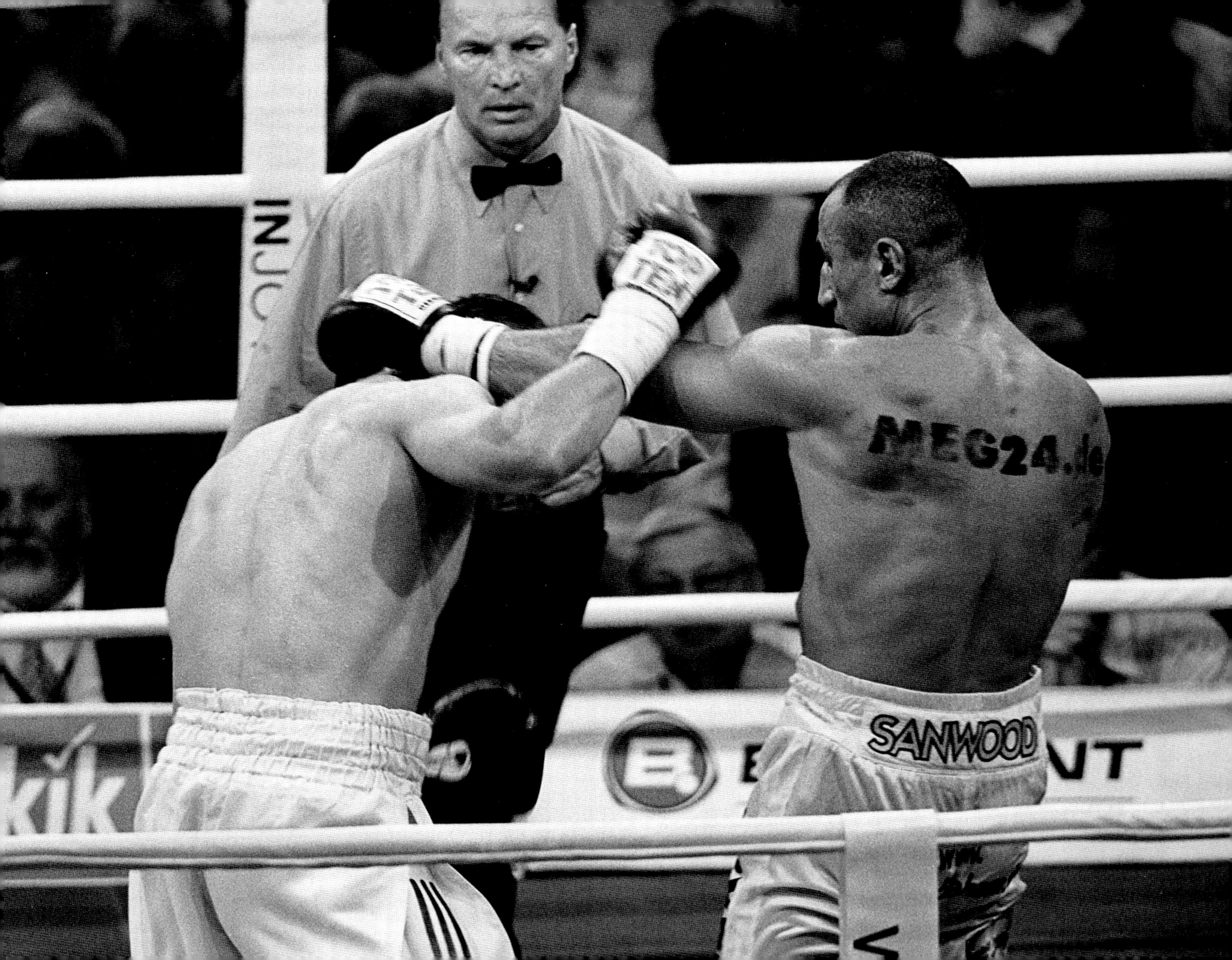
MEG24
SANWOOD

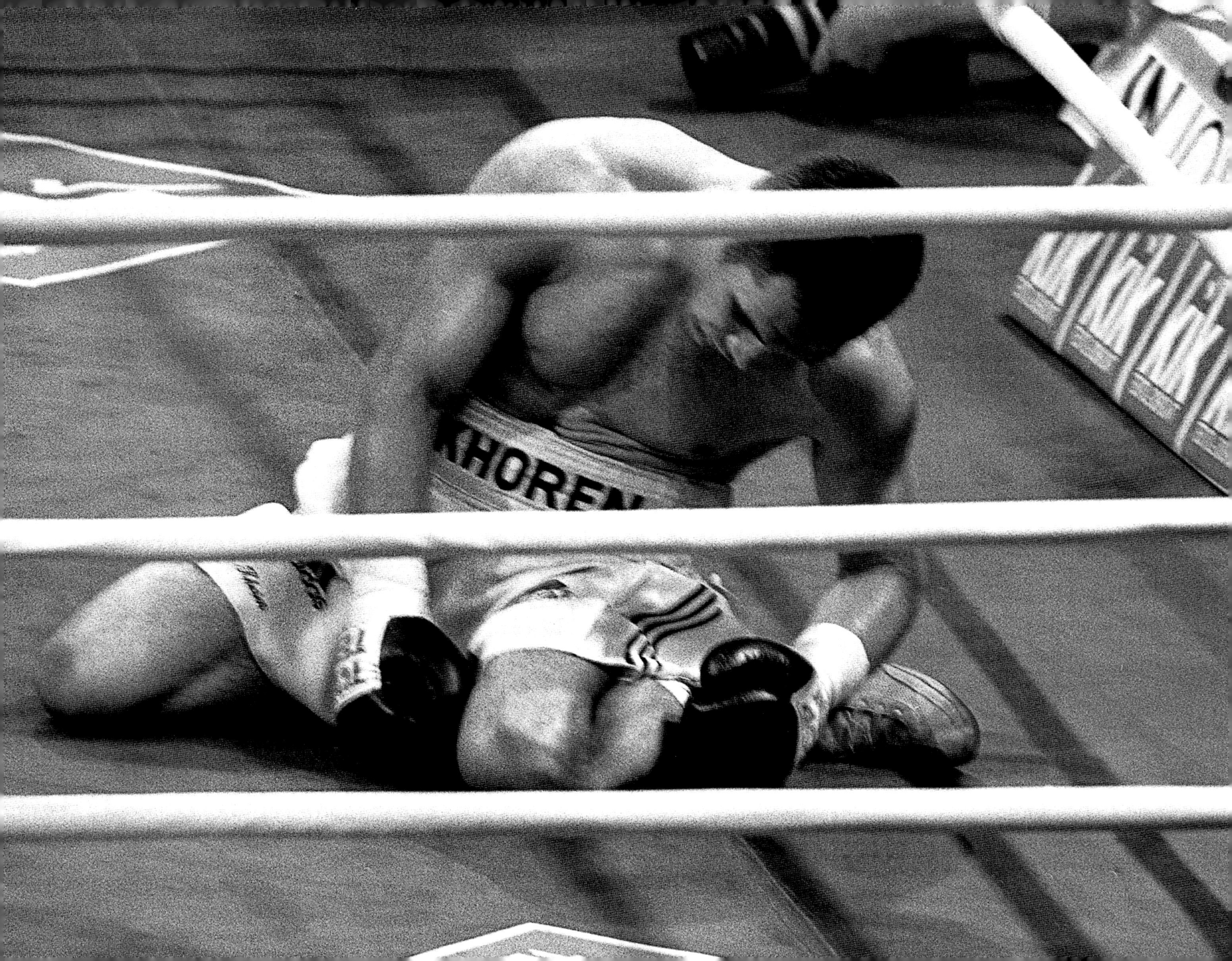
KHOREN

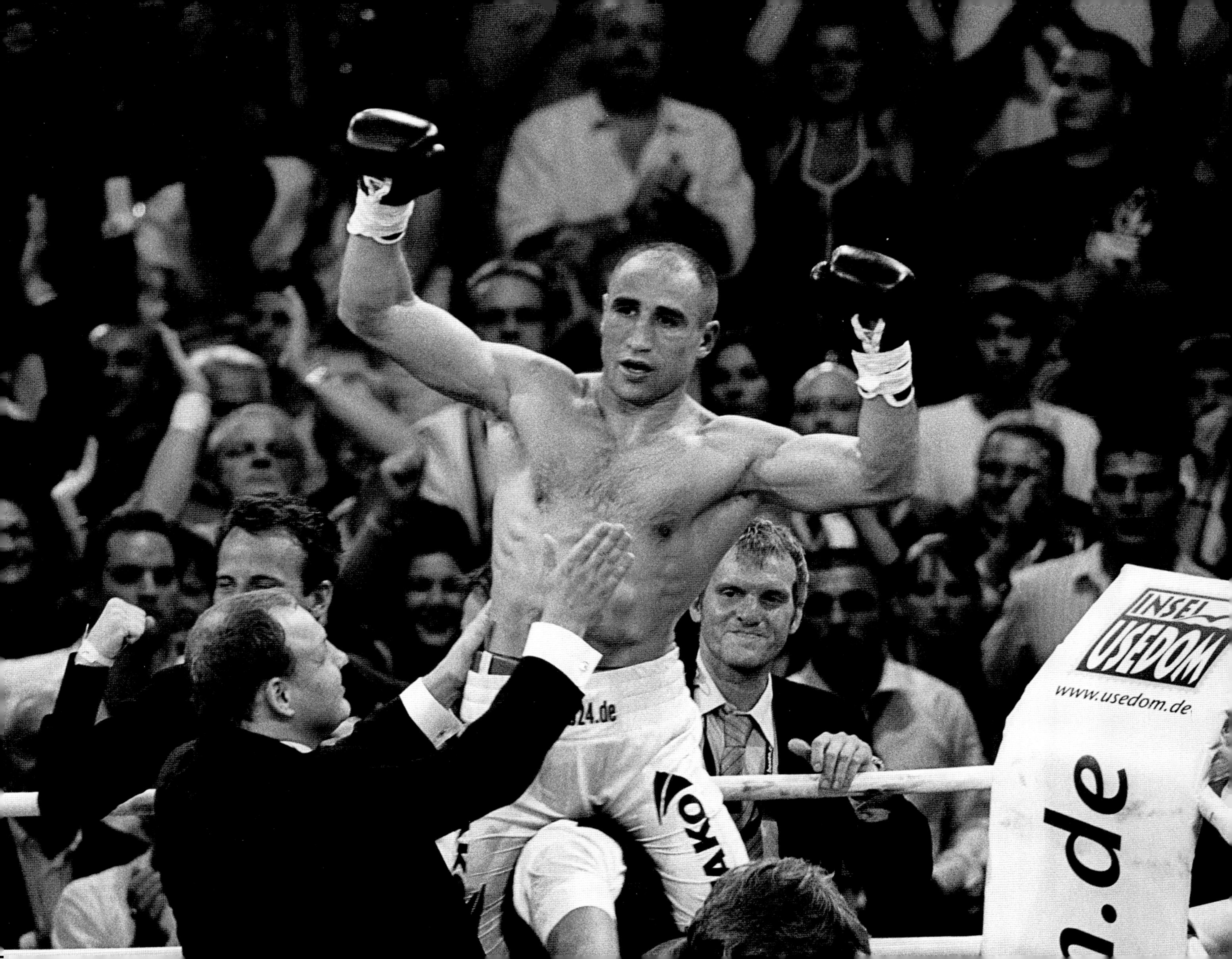
INSEL
USEDOM
www.usedom.de

Arthur Abraham vs Wayne Elcock
IBF middleweight title
08.12.2007 St. Jakob Halle
Basel, Schweiz
Fotos: Werner Dittmair

Die Angst durch einen Kopfstoß verursachten Cut am linken Auge nichts mehr sehen zu können beflügelten Arthur Abraham nach 4 verhalten geboxten Runden. Durch eine sauber und hart geschlagene Rechte ging Elcock in der 5. Runde zu Boden .Dieser kämpfte nochmal weiter aber vergeblich da der Ringrichter ihn durch Abbruch des Kampfes vor dem endgültigen K.o. des trotz angebrochener Rippe nun hart boxenden Abraham bewahrte.

Fears about not being able to see again after receiving a cut to the left eye following a headbutt occupied Arthur Abraham's thoughts during a restrained first four rounds. Elcock then went to ground after receiving a clean and hard right-hand blow in the fifth round. He got up to fight on, but the referee saved him from the eventual knockout by ending the fight against Abraham, who was still fighting hard despite having a fractured rib.

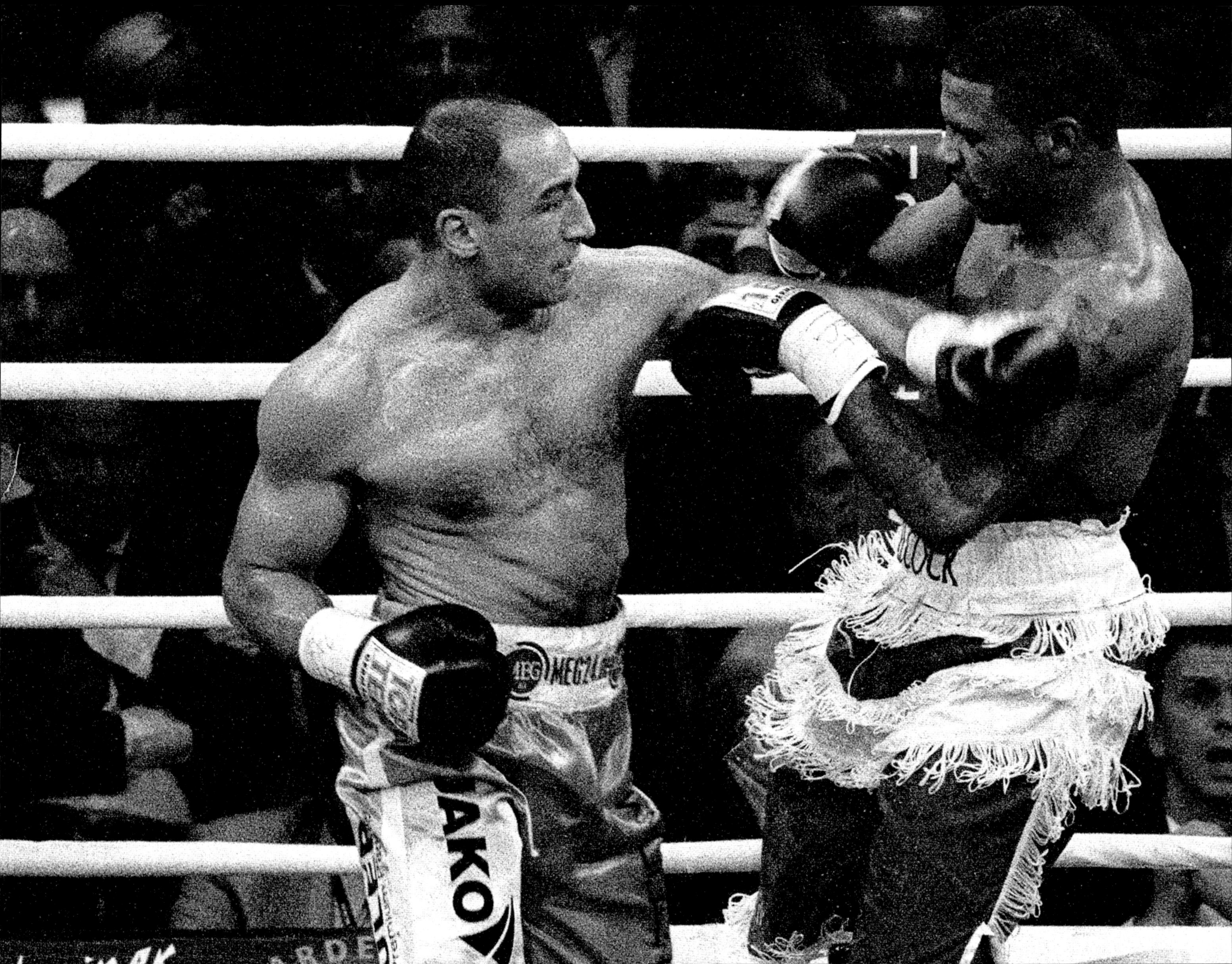
JAKO

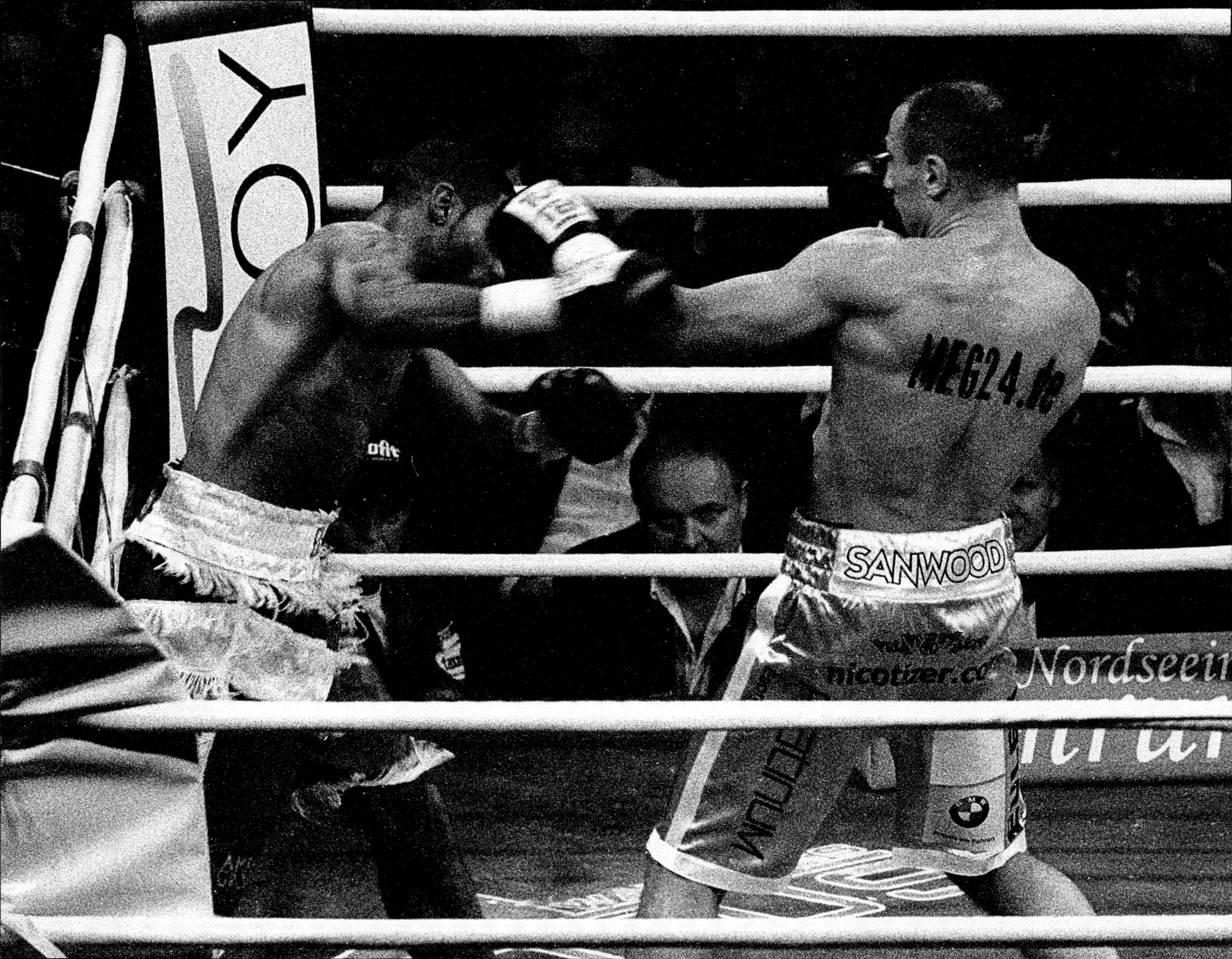
MEG24.de
SANWOOD

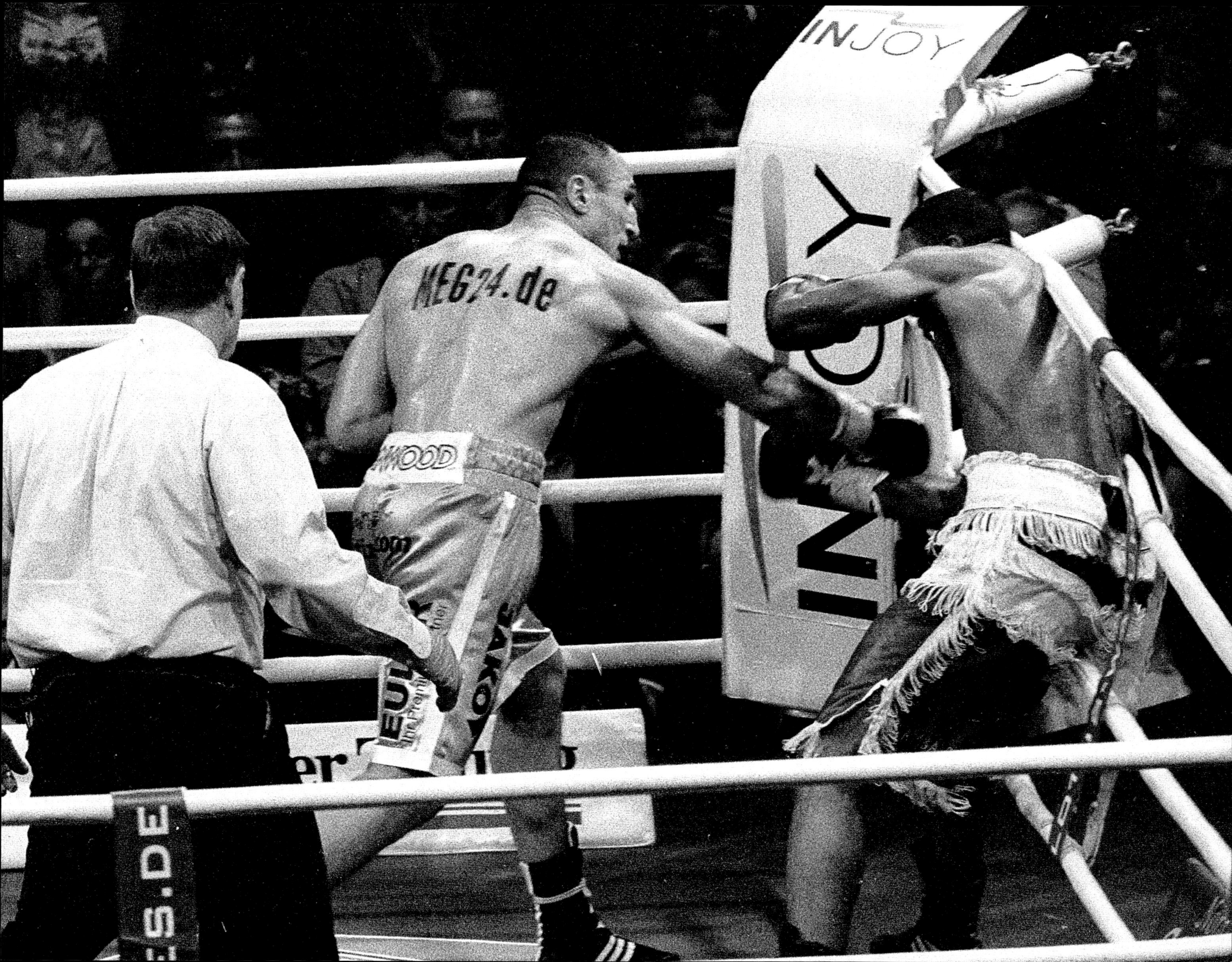
INJOY

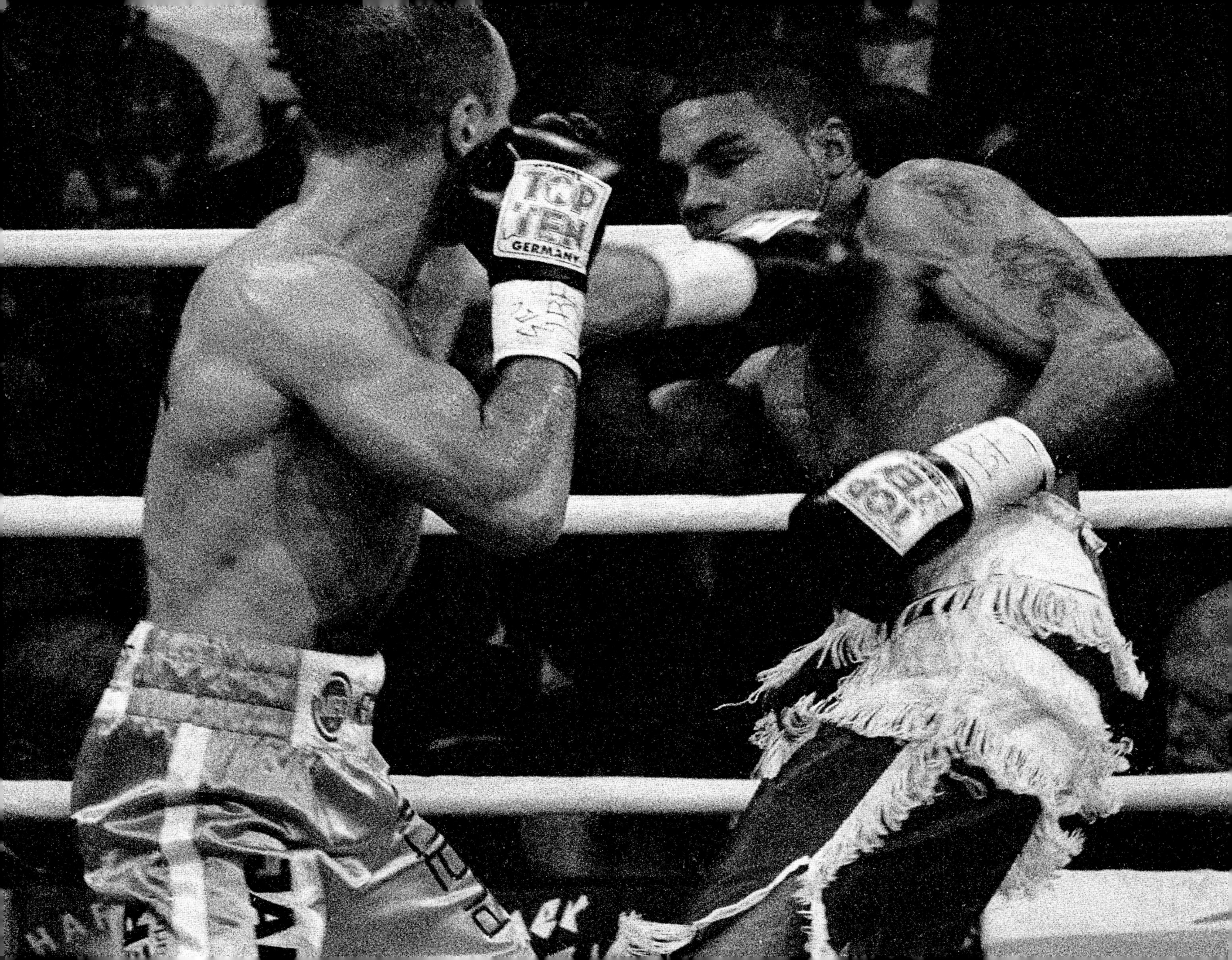
TOP TEN
GERMANY

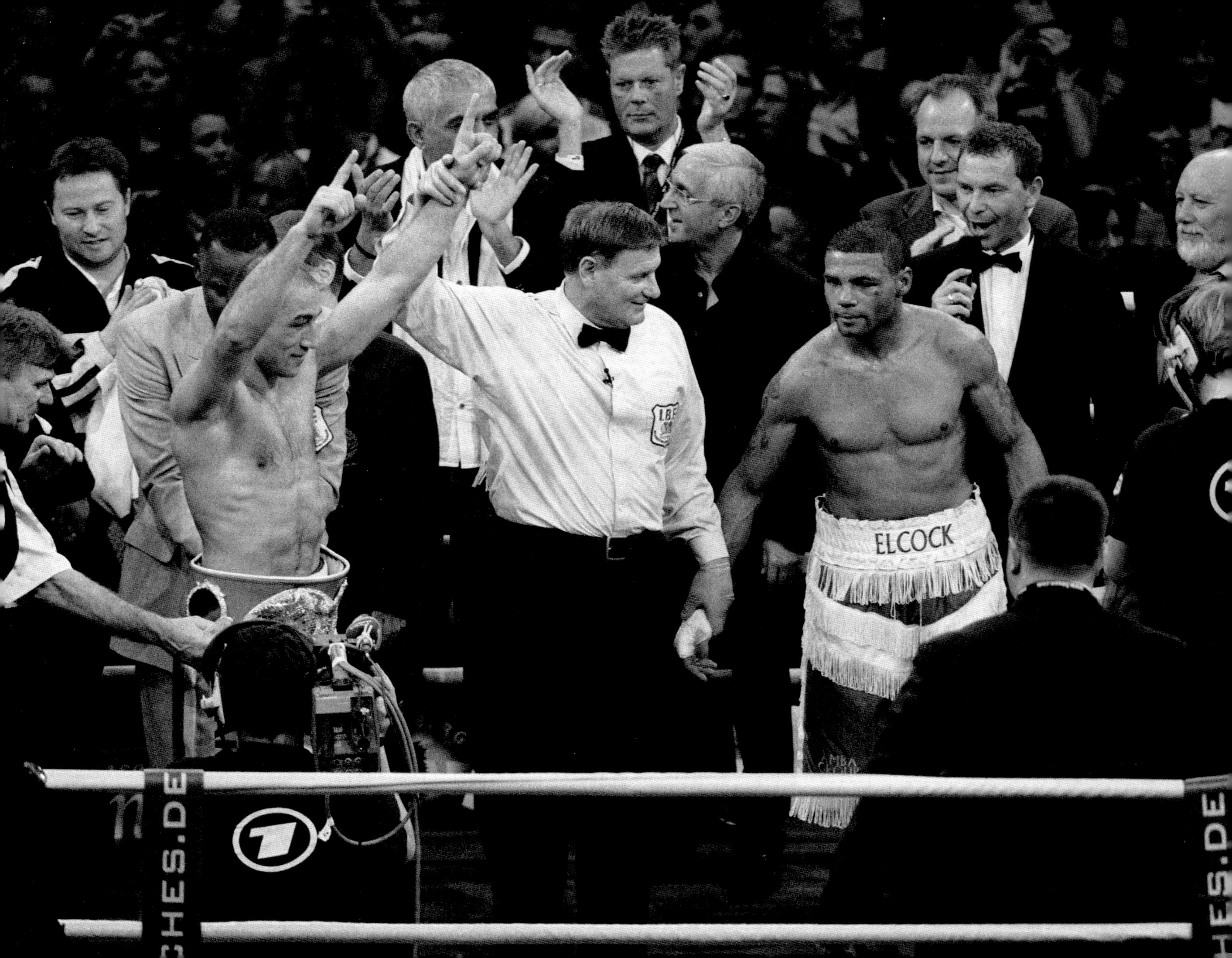
ELCOCK

Arthur Abraham vs Elvin Ayala
IBF middleweight title
29.03.2008 Sparkassen-Arena
Kiel, Deutschland
Fotos: Werner Dittmair

Auch in der 7. Titelverteidigung boxte Arthur Abraham in der gewohnten Manier. Nach verhaltenem Start ging Ayala in der 5. Runde trotz unglaublicher Nehmerqualitäten, erstmals zu Boden. In der 7. und 11. Runde machte Ayala erheblich Druck auf Abraham. Mit einer Linken zum Kinn, schickte Abraham den Gegner in der 12. Runde auf die Bretter des Rings. Wieder ein KNOCKOUT!

Arthur Abraham boxed in his usual manner also for his seventh title defence. After a restrained start, Ayala went to the ground for the first time in the fifth round, despite showing incredible resistance. In the seventh and 11th rounds, Ayala put immense pressure on Abraham. With a left-hander to the chin, Abraham sent his opponent crashing to the floor in the 12th round. Another KNOCKOUT!

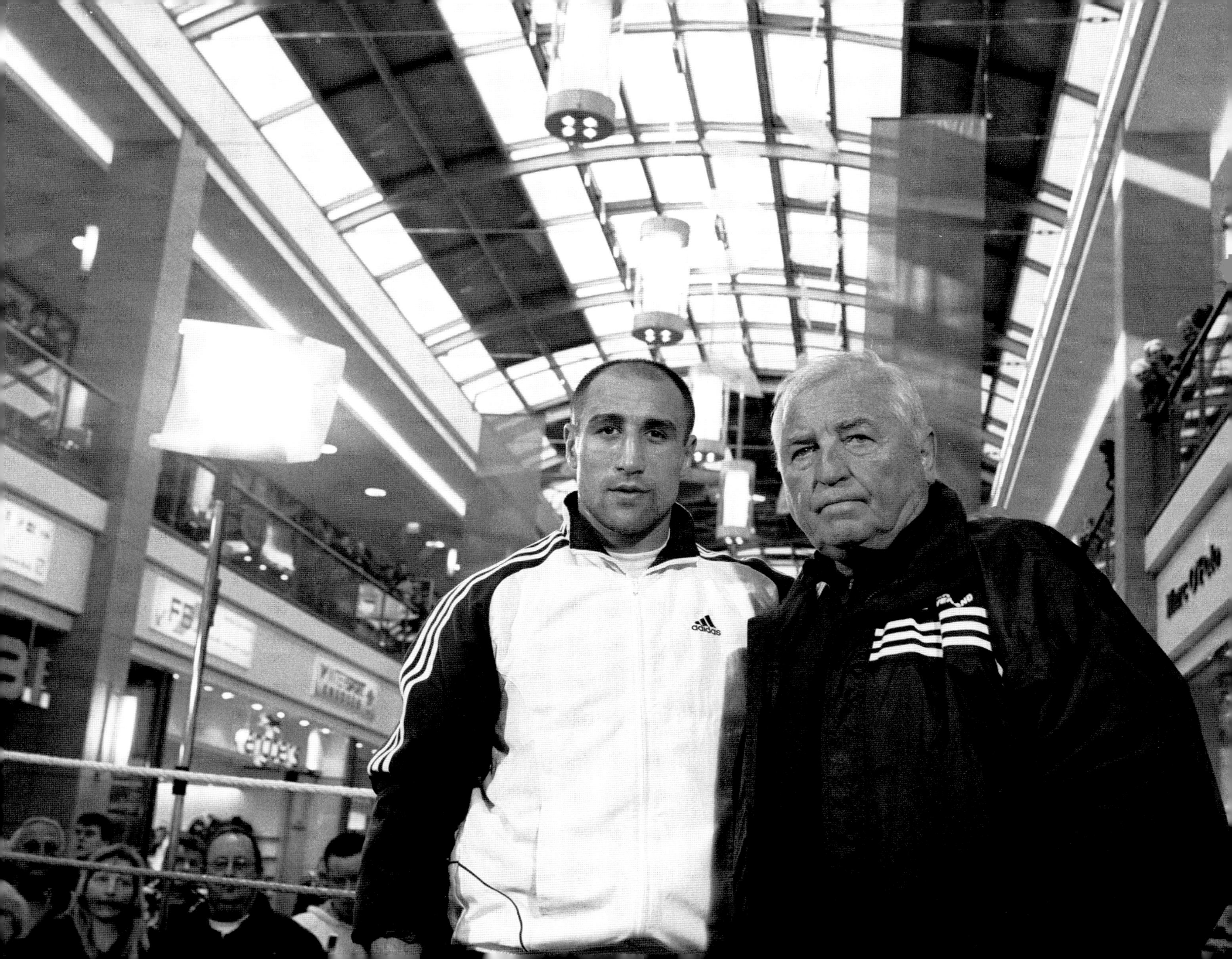
adidas

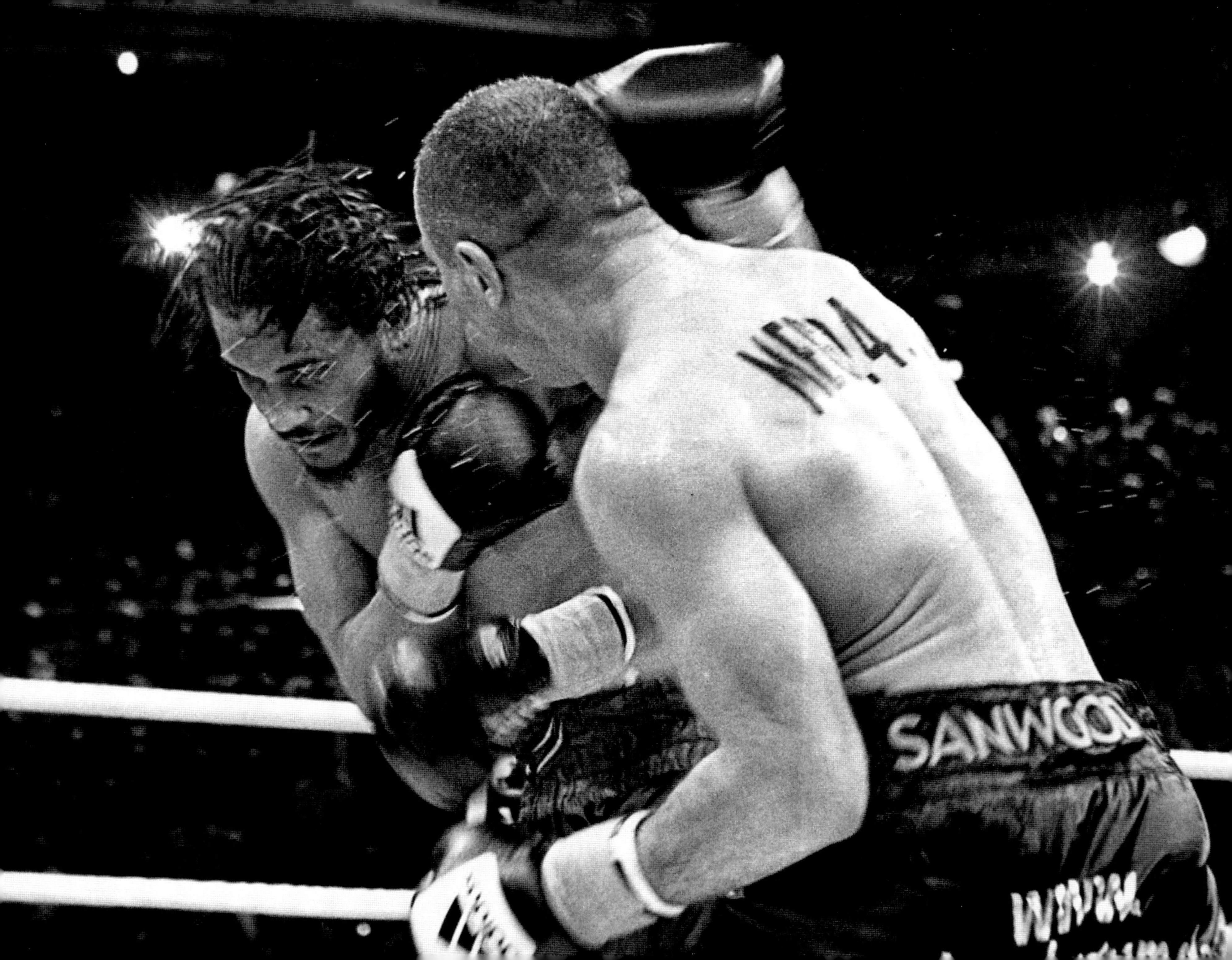

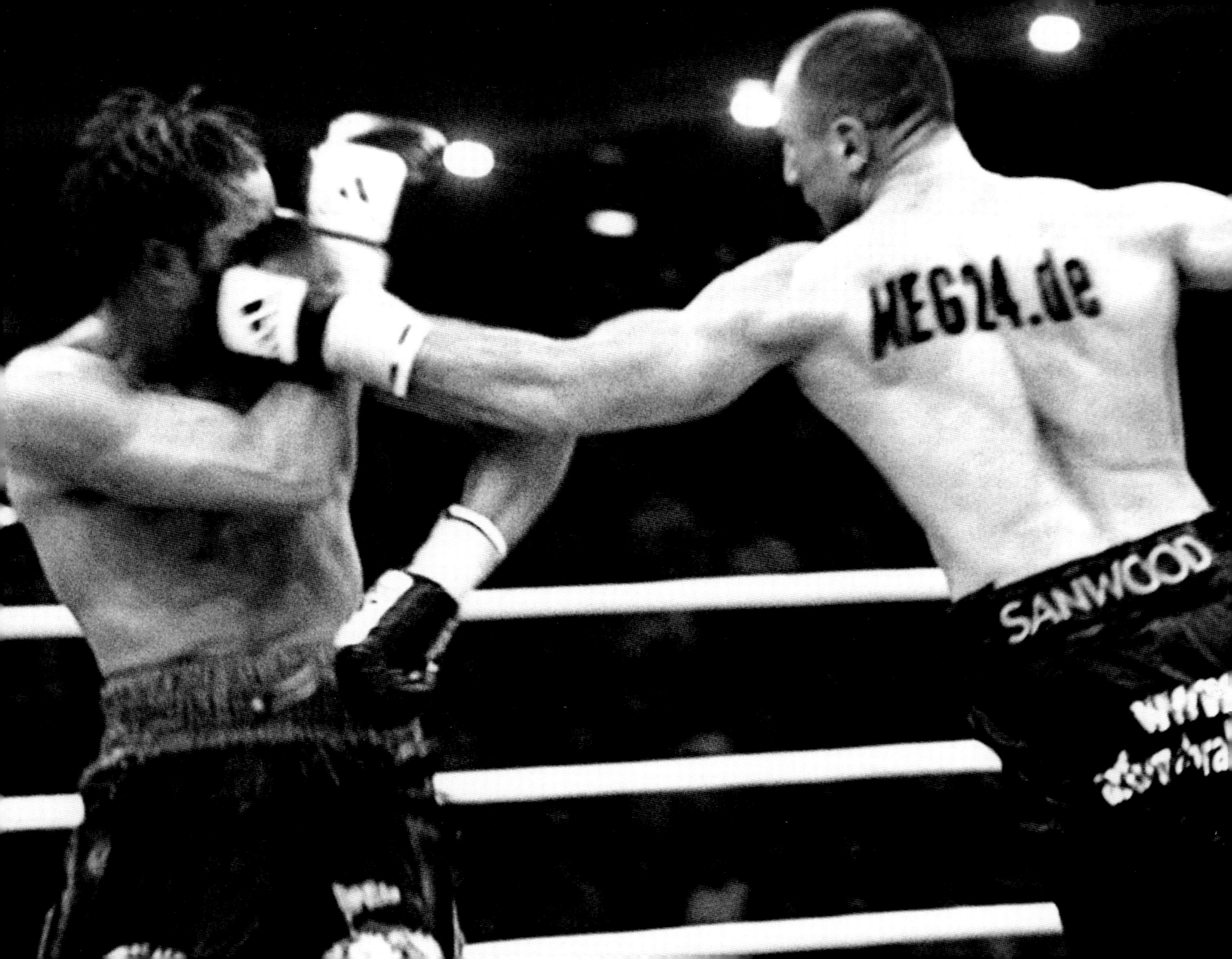
HEG24.de
SANWOOD

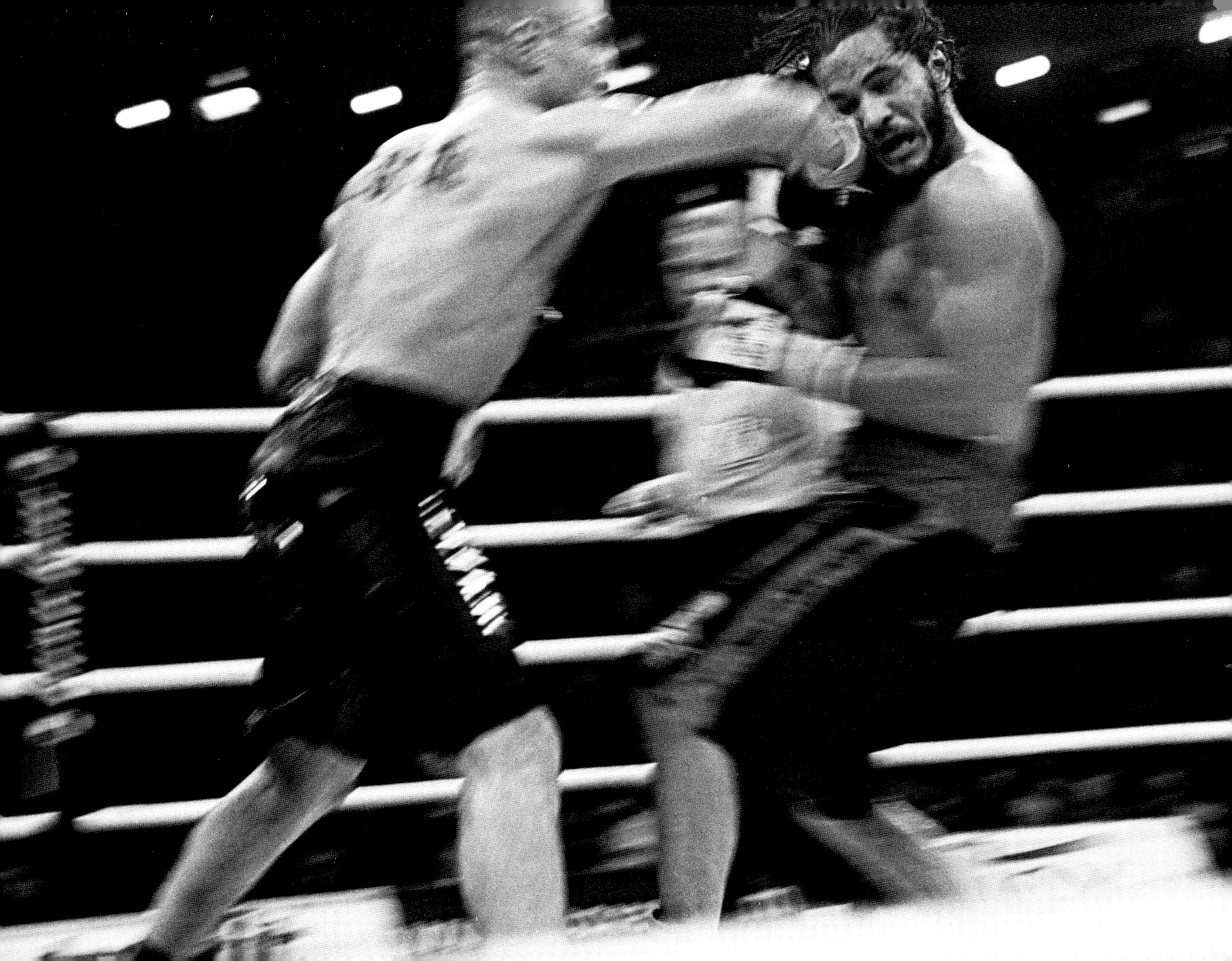

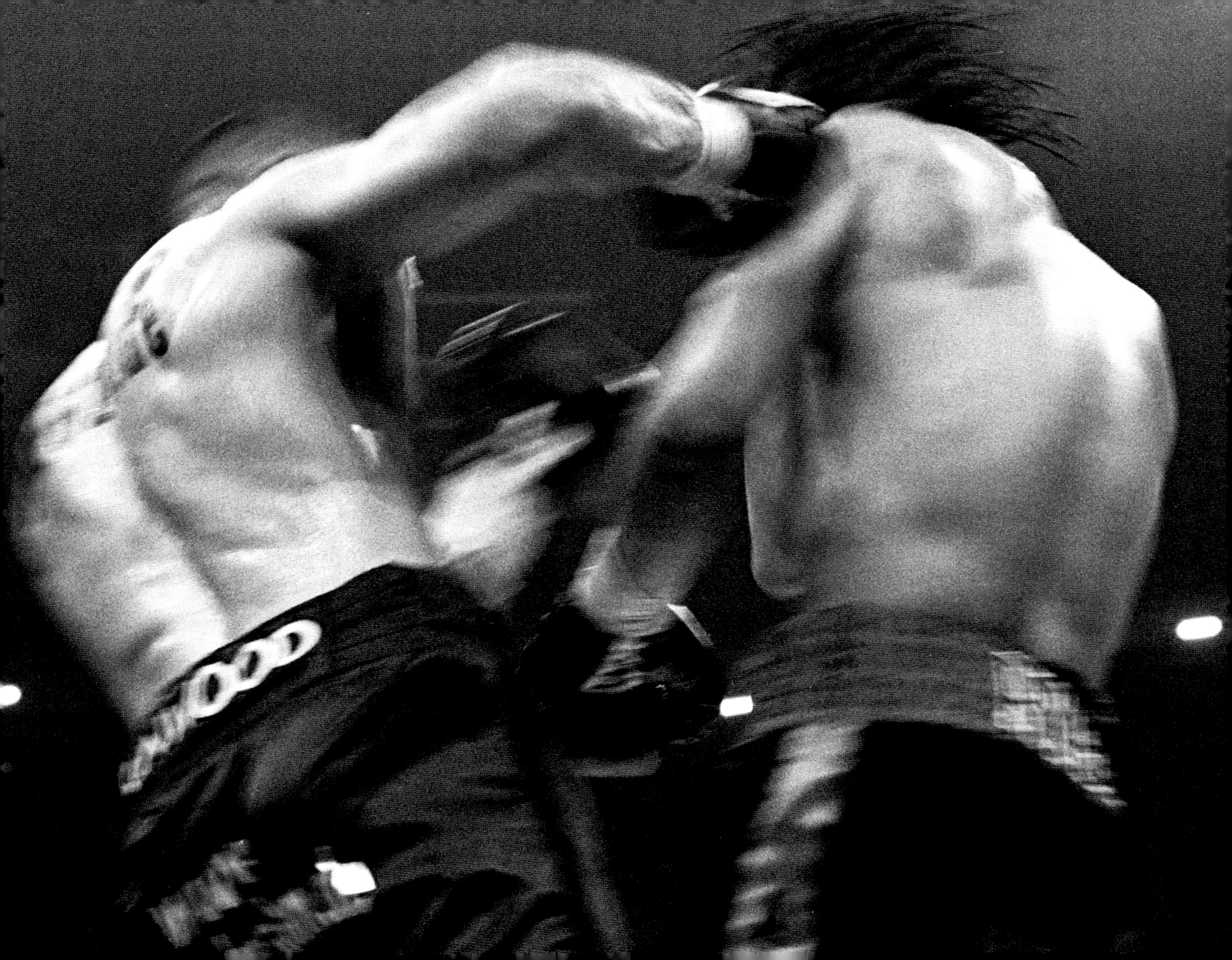

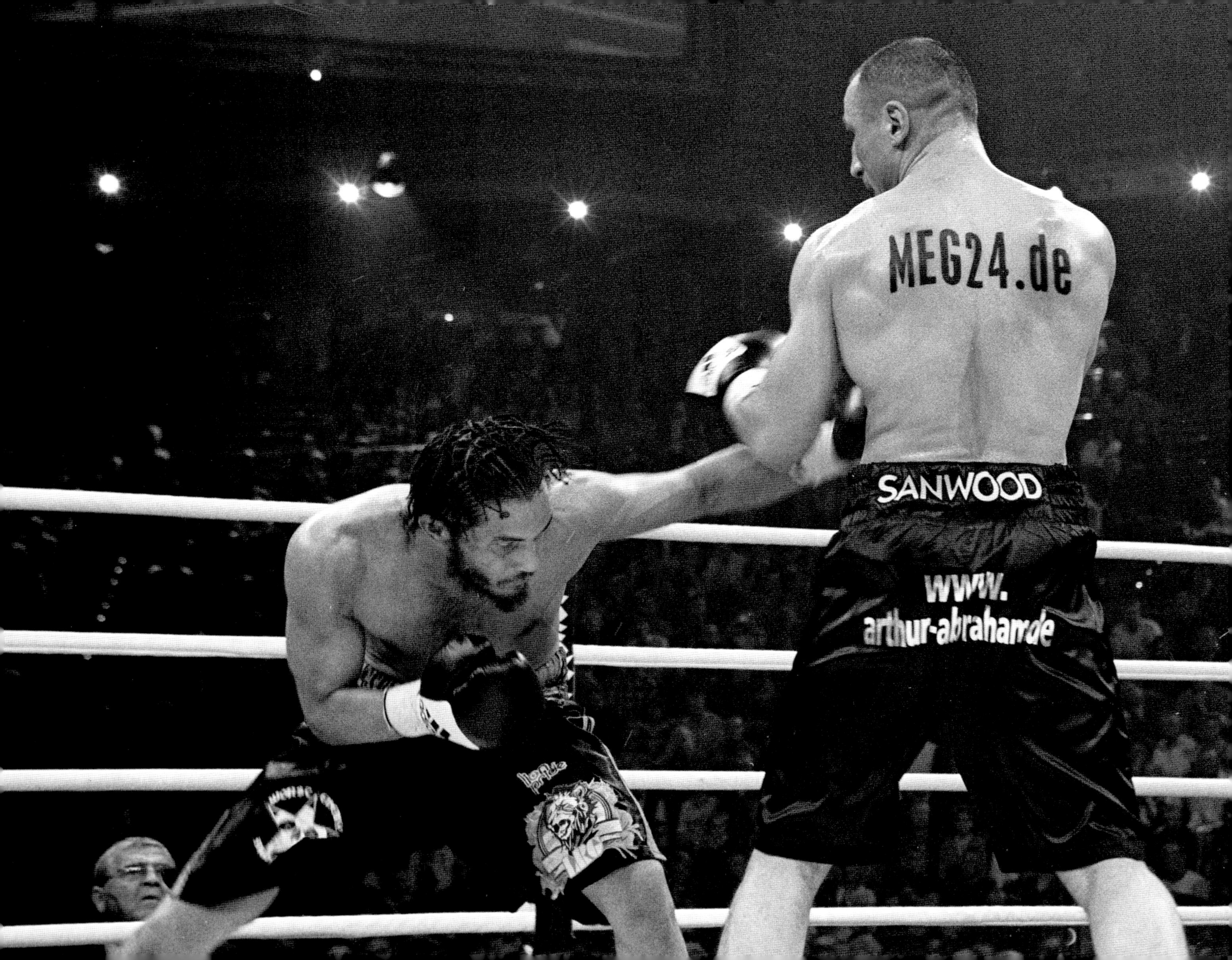
MEG24.de
SANWOOD
www.
arthur-abrahamde

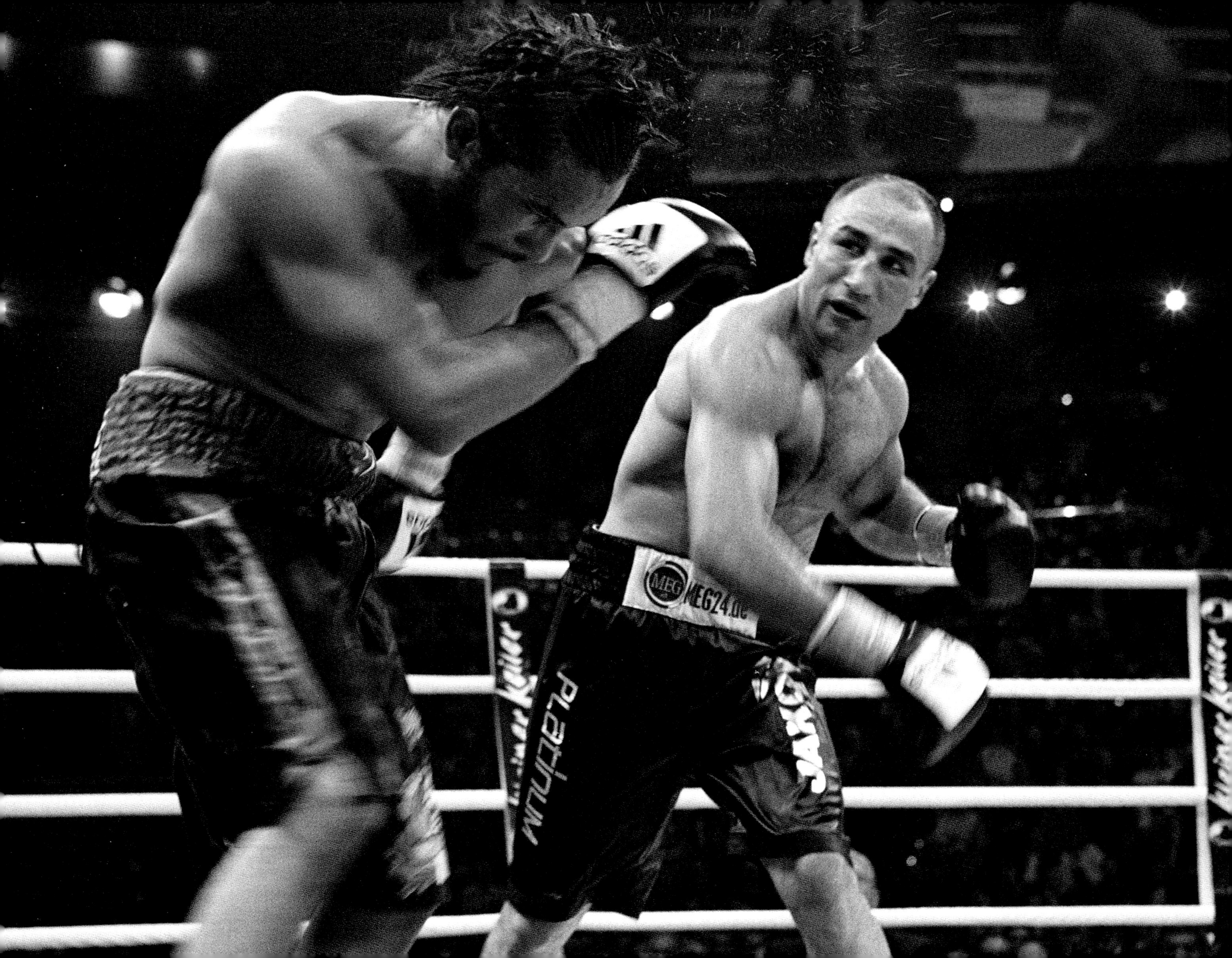
MEG
MEG24.de
Platinum

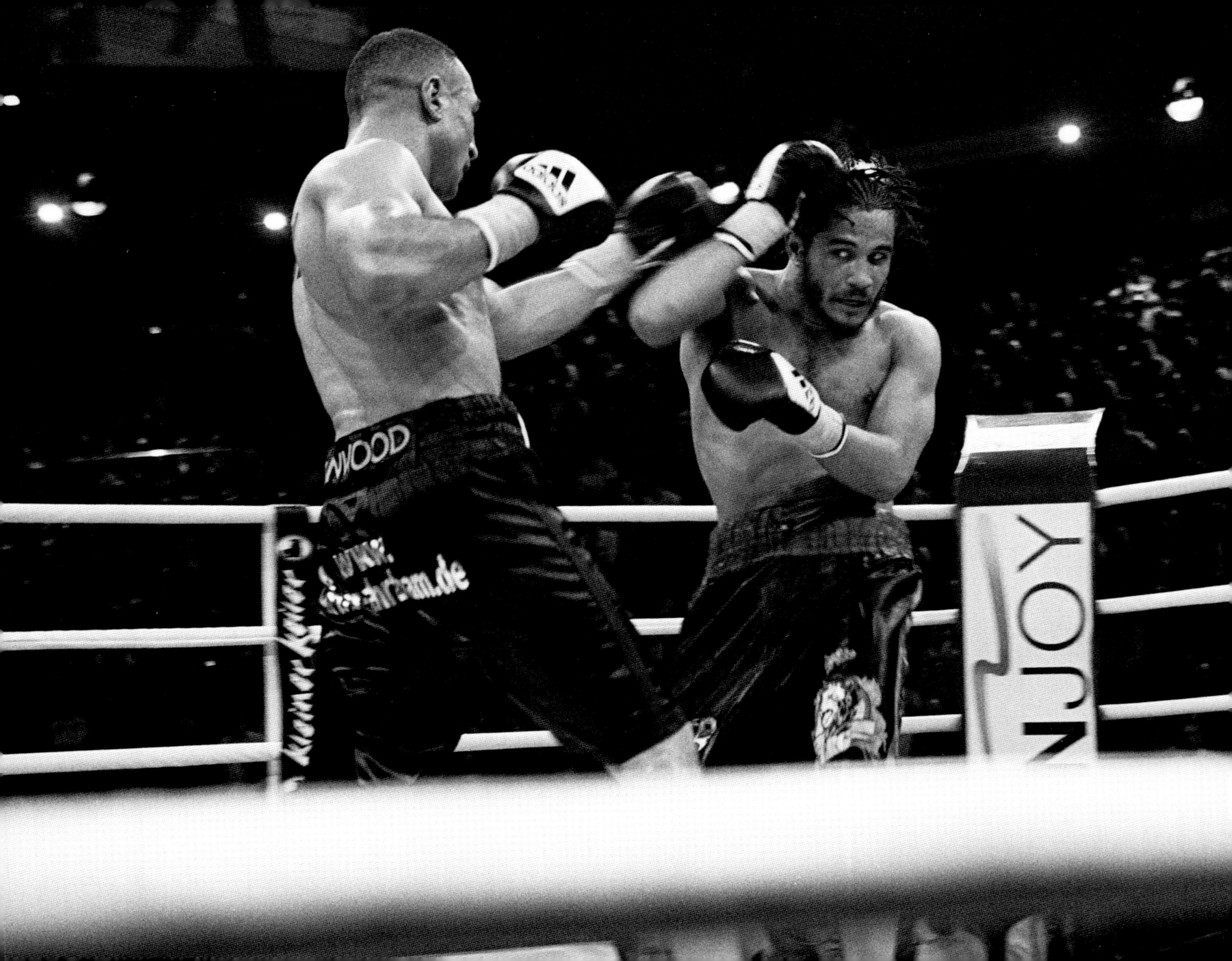

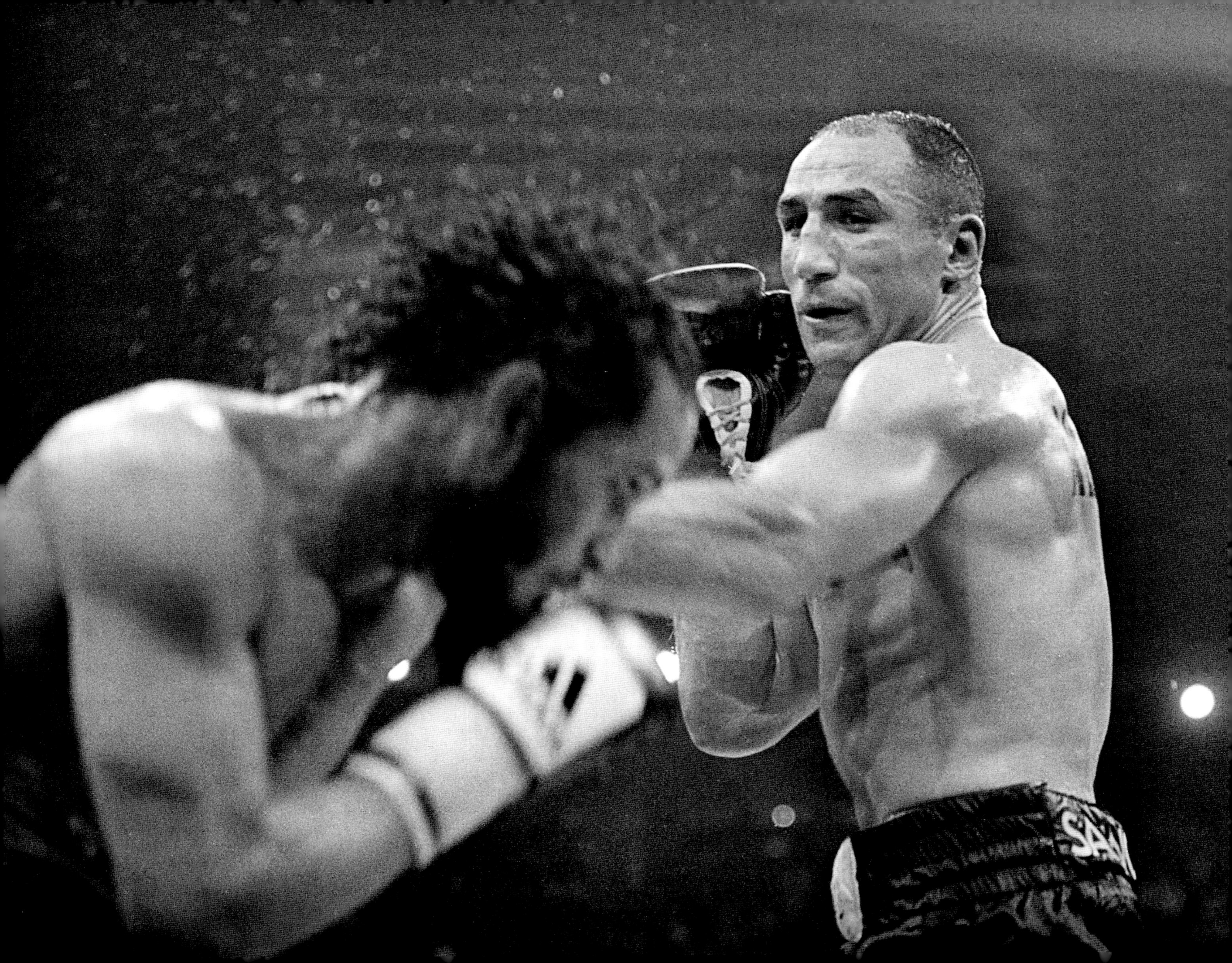

Elvin Ayala , Arthur und Vater Gregor Abraham

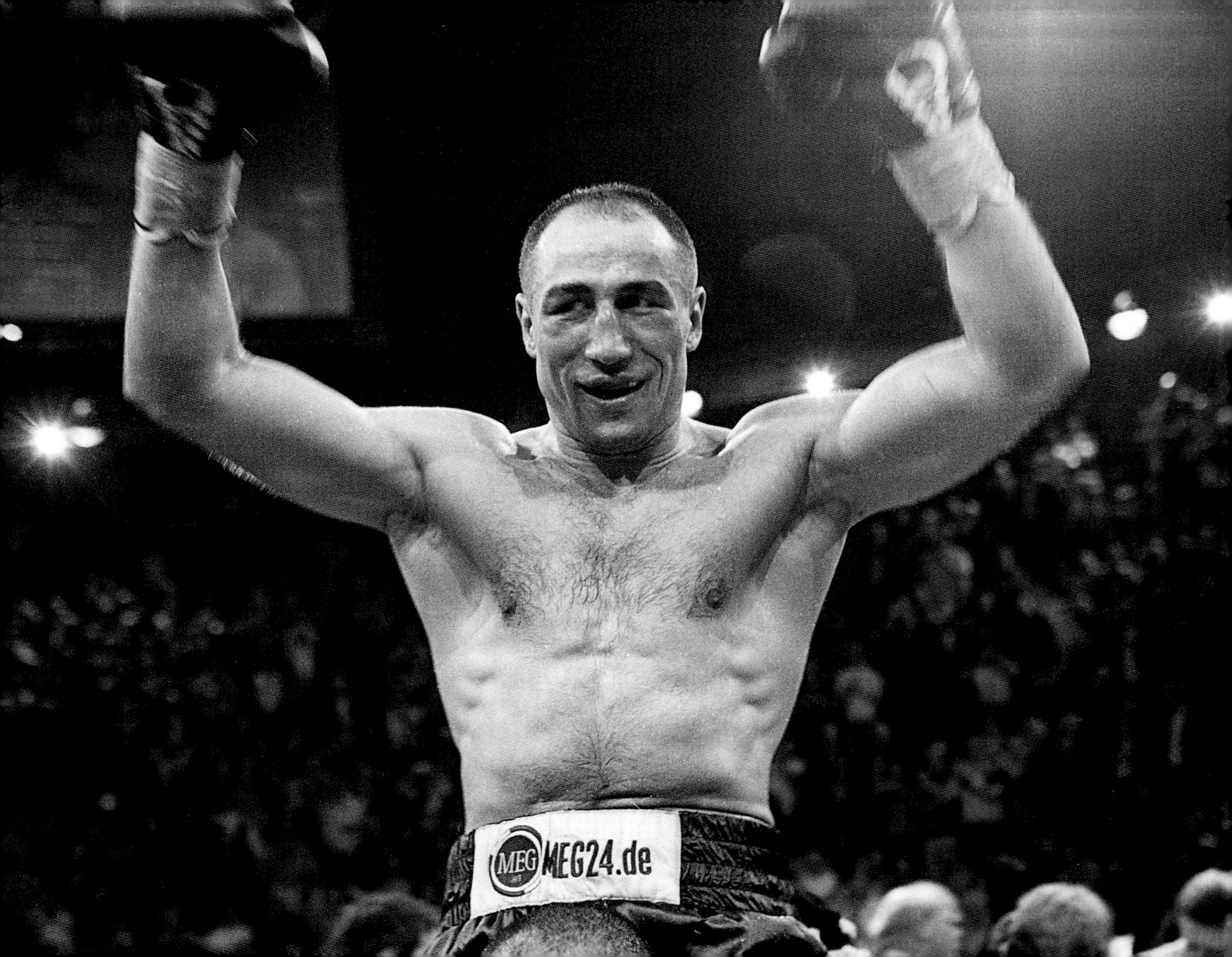
MEG
MEG24.de

Arthur Abraham vs Edison Miranda
"Die Rache"
21.06.2008 Seminole Hard Rock
Hotel & Casino
Hollywood, Florida, USA
Fotos: Werner Dittmair

Sonne pur, gute Laune und die fantastische Landschaft waren in Hollywood, FLORIDA ein Teil der finalen Vorbereitung für die Vergeltung der Schlacht von Wetzlar gegen Edison MIRANDA. Nach Plan provozierend und mit Doppeldeckung boxend überließ Arthur Abraham die ersten 3 Runden dem Kolumbianer. Dieser Boxstil ist in Amerika nicht sehr beliebt und Abraham musste Buhrufe des Publikums wegen Untätigkeit einstecken. In der 4. Runde bestrafte ABRAHAM endlich den Panther mit drei Niederschlägen. Der in der Pressekonferenz großmäulig aufgetretenen MIRANDA musste nach dem Kampf seine Meinung über ABRAHAM gewaltig revidieren. Dieser Kampf war der einzige welcher nicht als Titelverteidigung galt und deshalb außerhalb des Gewichtslimits des Mittelgewichts stattfand.

Sun, high spirits and fantastic scenery made Hollywood, FLORIDA, a part of the final preparations for avenging the slaughter of Wetzlar against Edison MIRANDA. Provocative, just according to plan, and boxing with a defence and counter tactic, Arthur Abraham let the Colombian take the first three rounds. This style of boxing is not very popular in America and Abraham had to accept the crowds' jeers for his idleness. In the fourth round, ABRAHAM finally punished the panther with three heavy blows. MIRANDA, who had been big mouthed during the press conference, was forced to significantly revise his opinion about ABRAHAM after the fight. This was the only fight which did not count as a title defence and, therefore, took place outside the Middleweight weight limits.

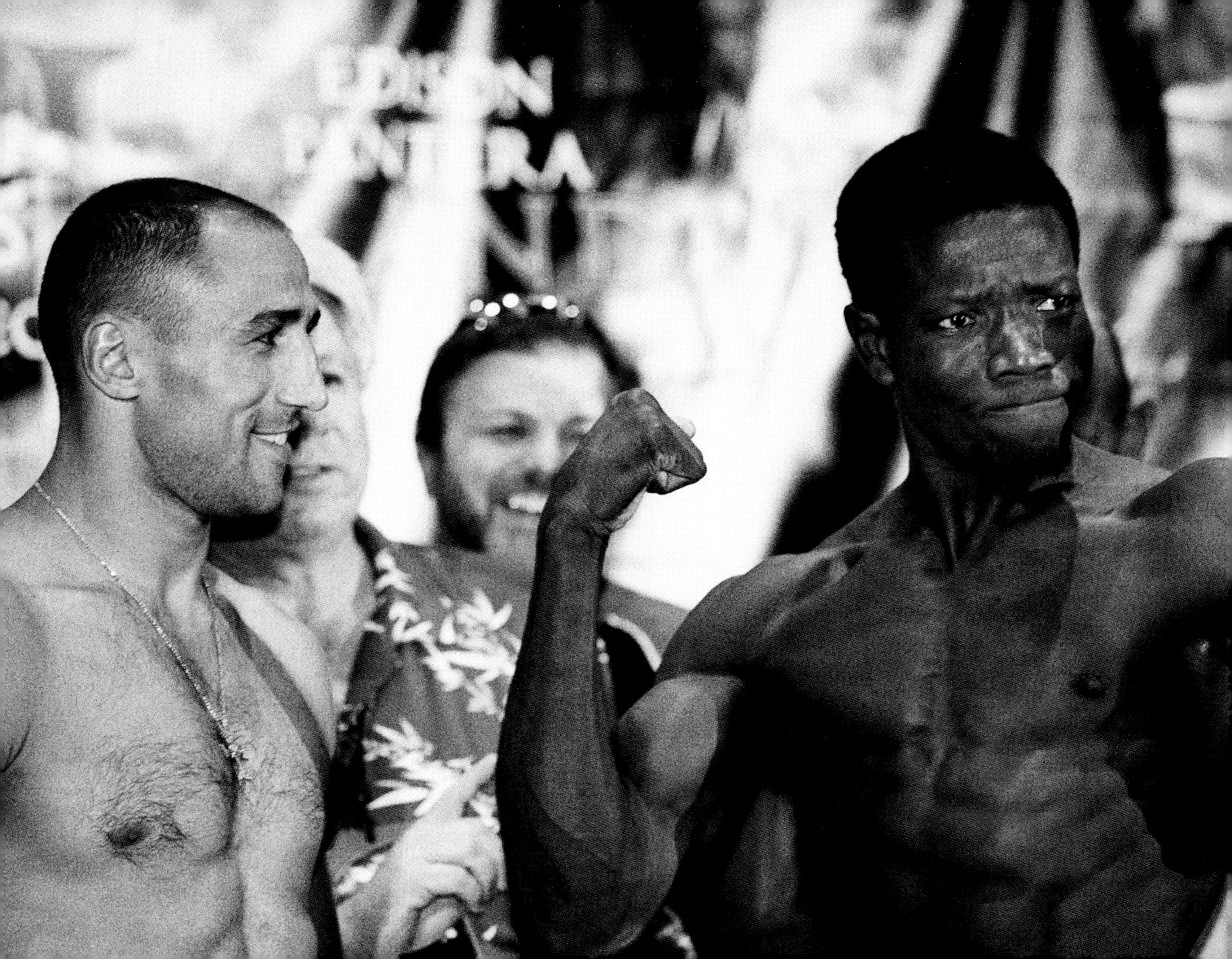

WORLD CLASS BOXING
Arthur
ABRAHAM
II
VS
Edison
MIRANDA
THE BATTLE CONTINUES...
JUNE 21
Hard Rock
LIVE
SEMINOLE HARD ROCK
HOTEL & CASINO
CBS
HOLLYWOOD SMOKE SHOP
IGARETTES
MAVERICK
$18.00
KOOL
SEMINOLE
WELCOME TO THE
HOLLYWOOD
SEMINOLE
RESERVATION
RESERVATION ESTABLISHED 1911

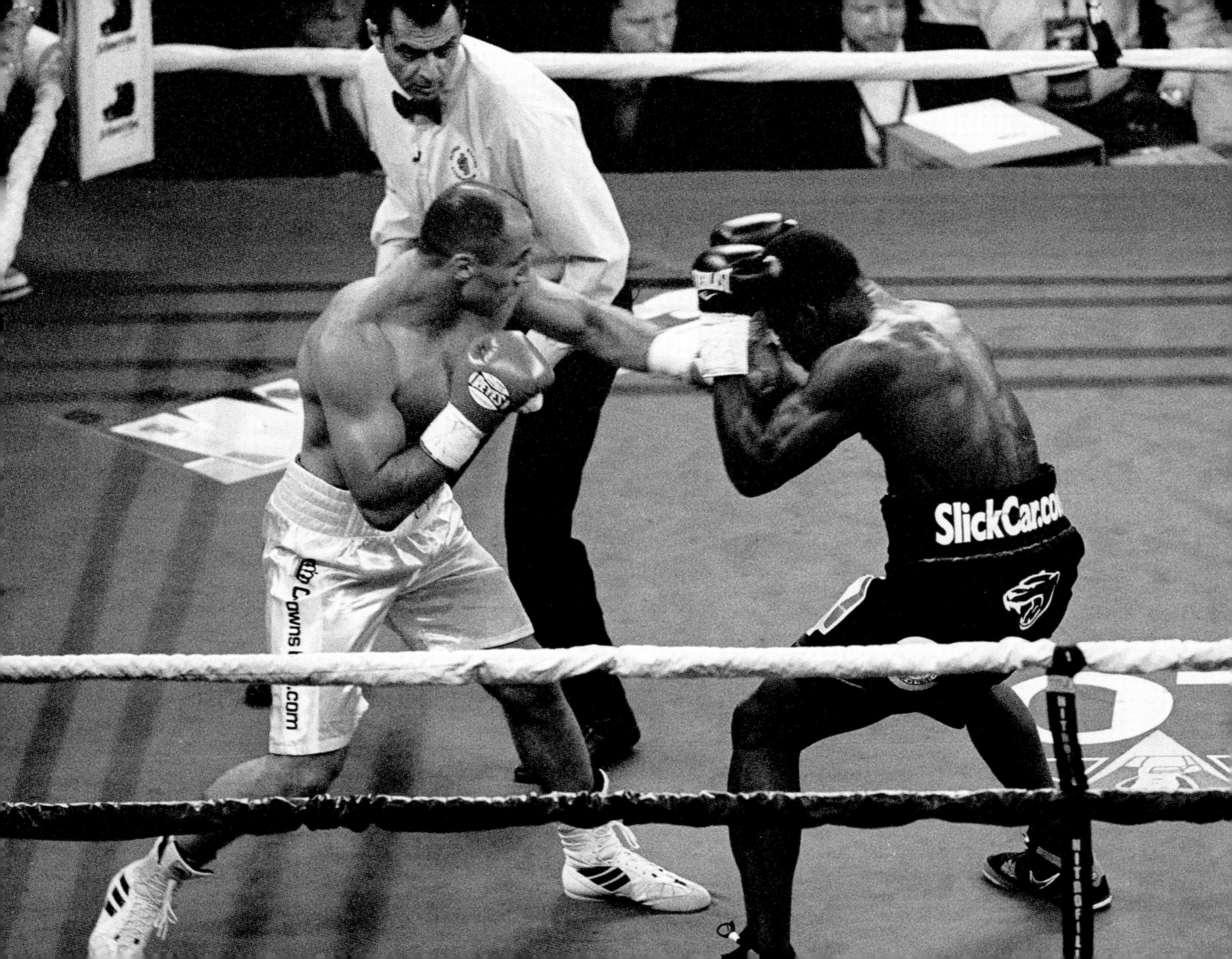
SlickCar.com

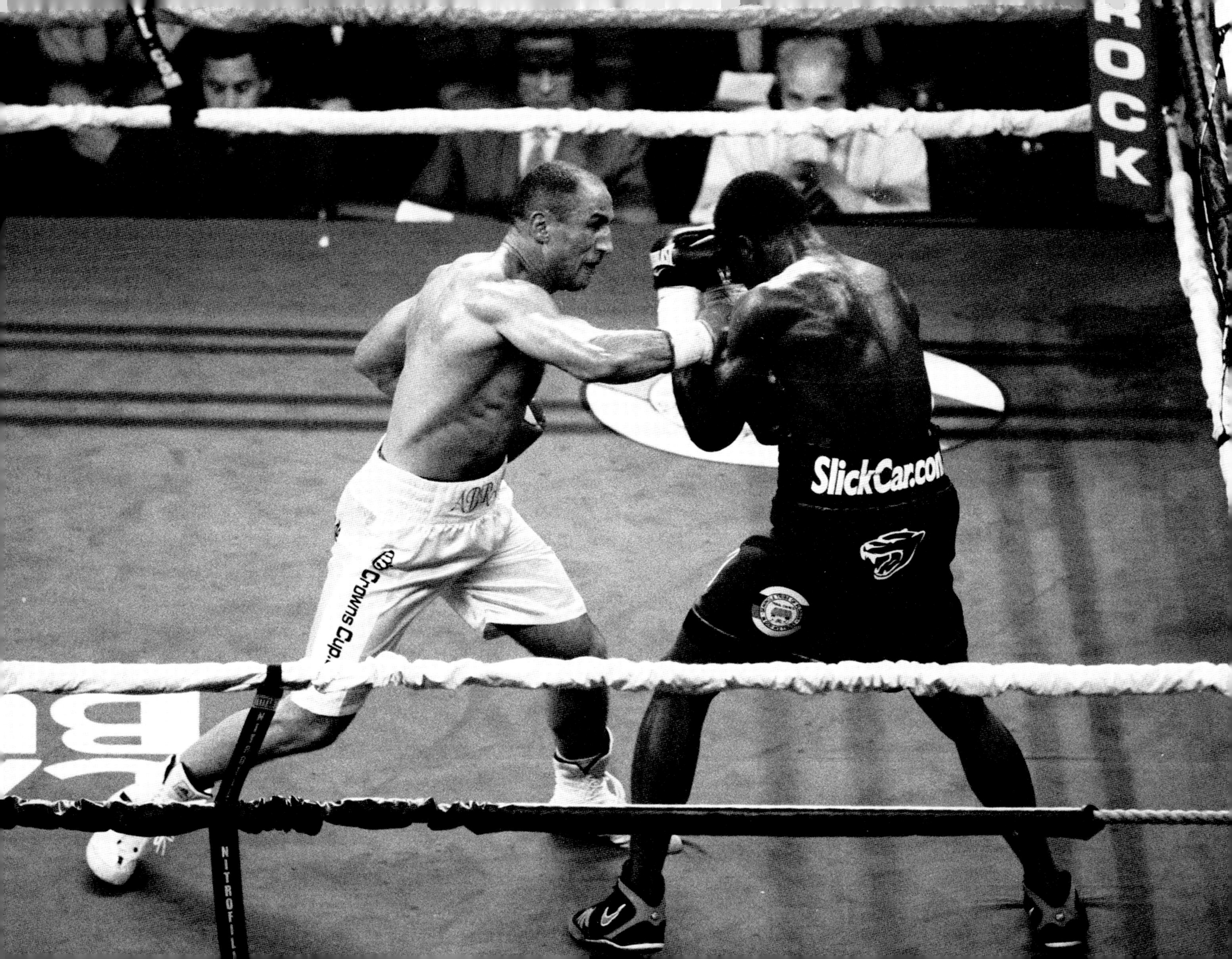
ROCK
SlickCar.com

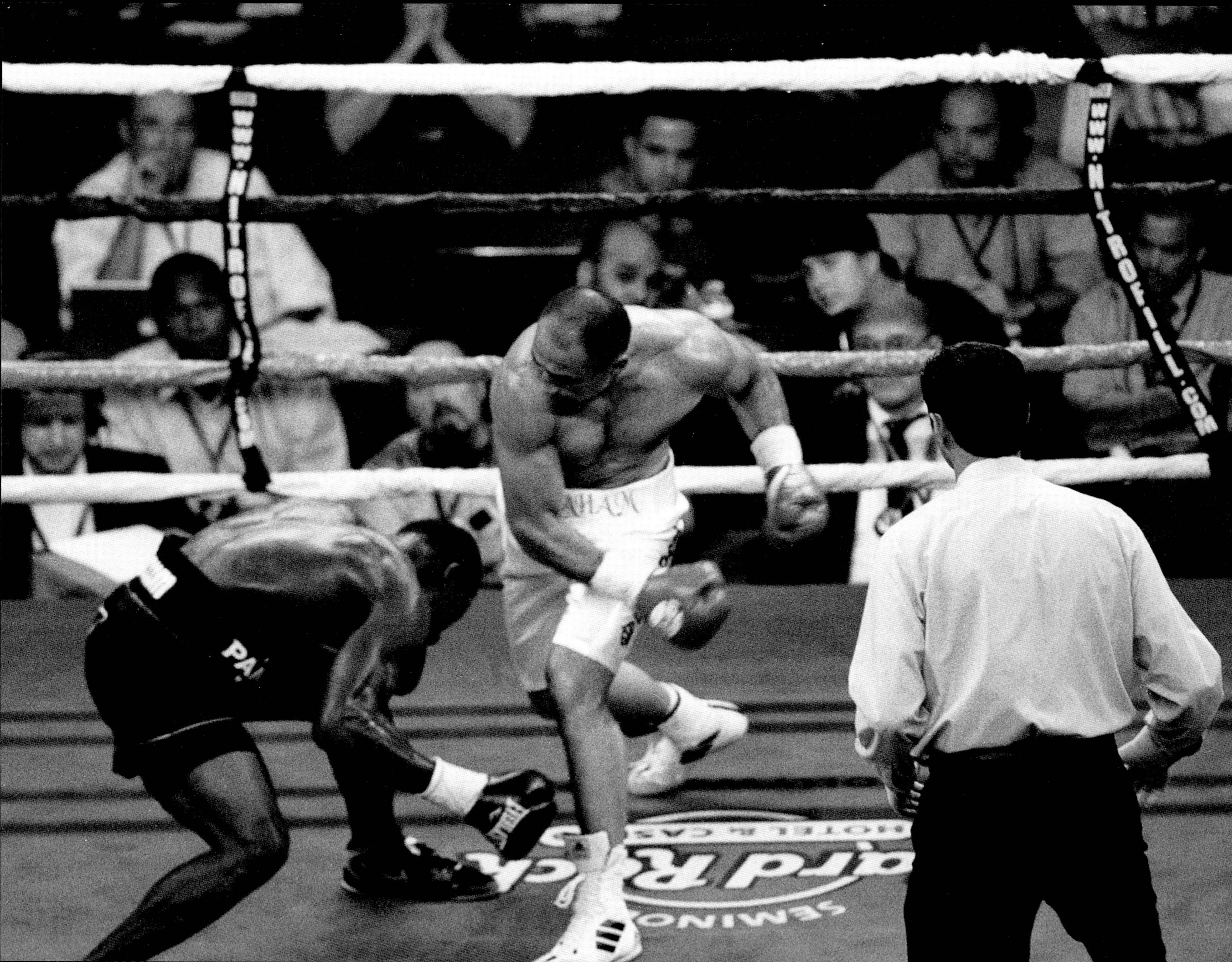
WWW.NITROBALL.COM

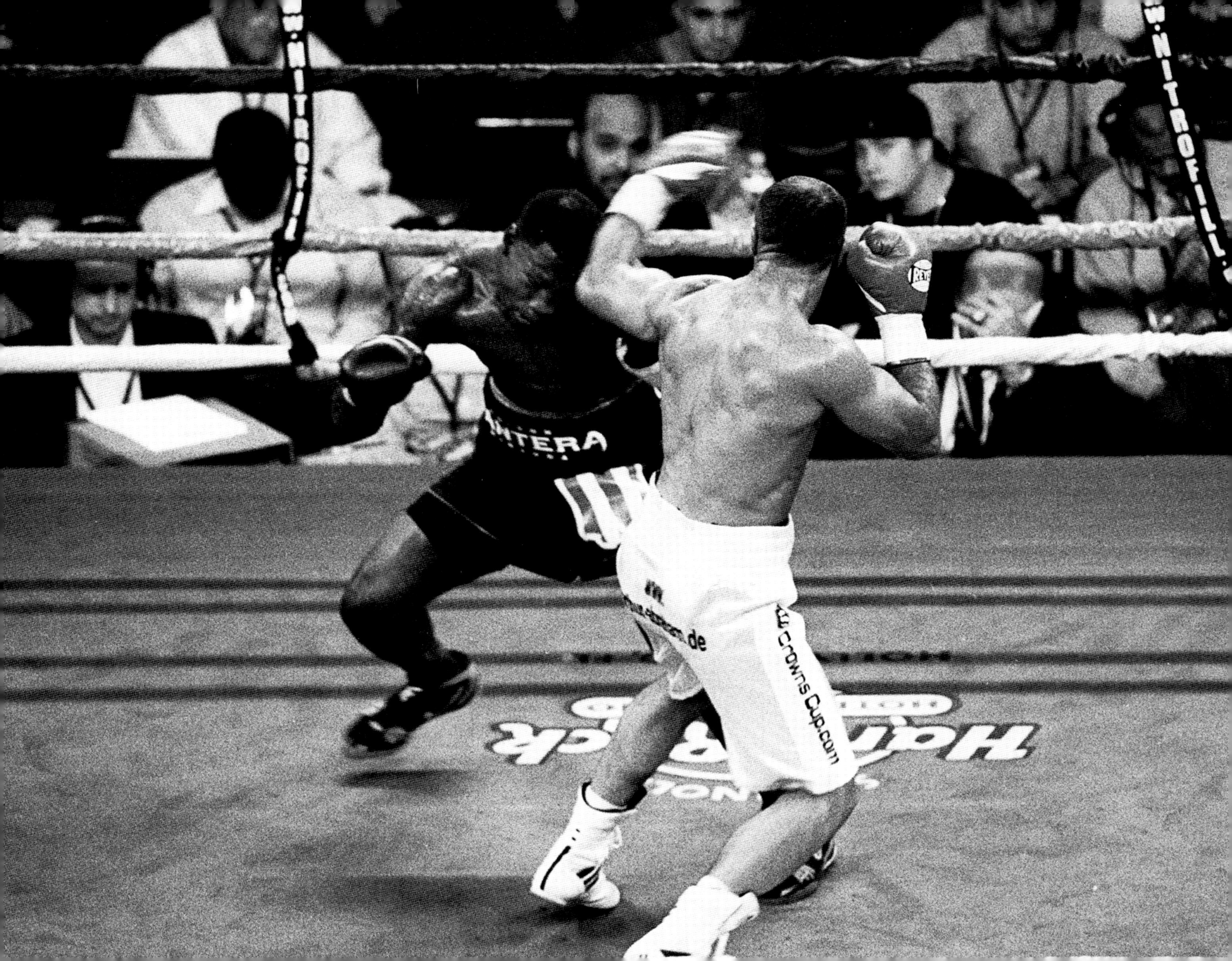
CrownsCup.com

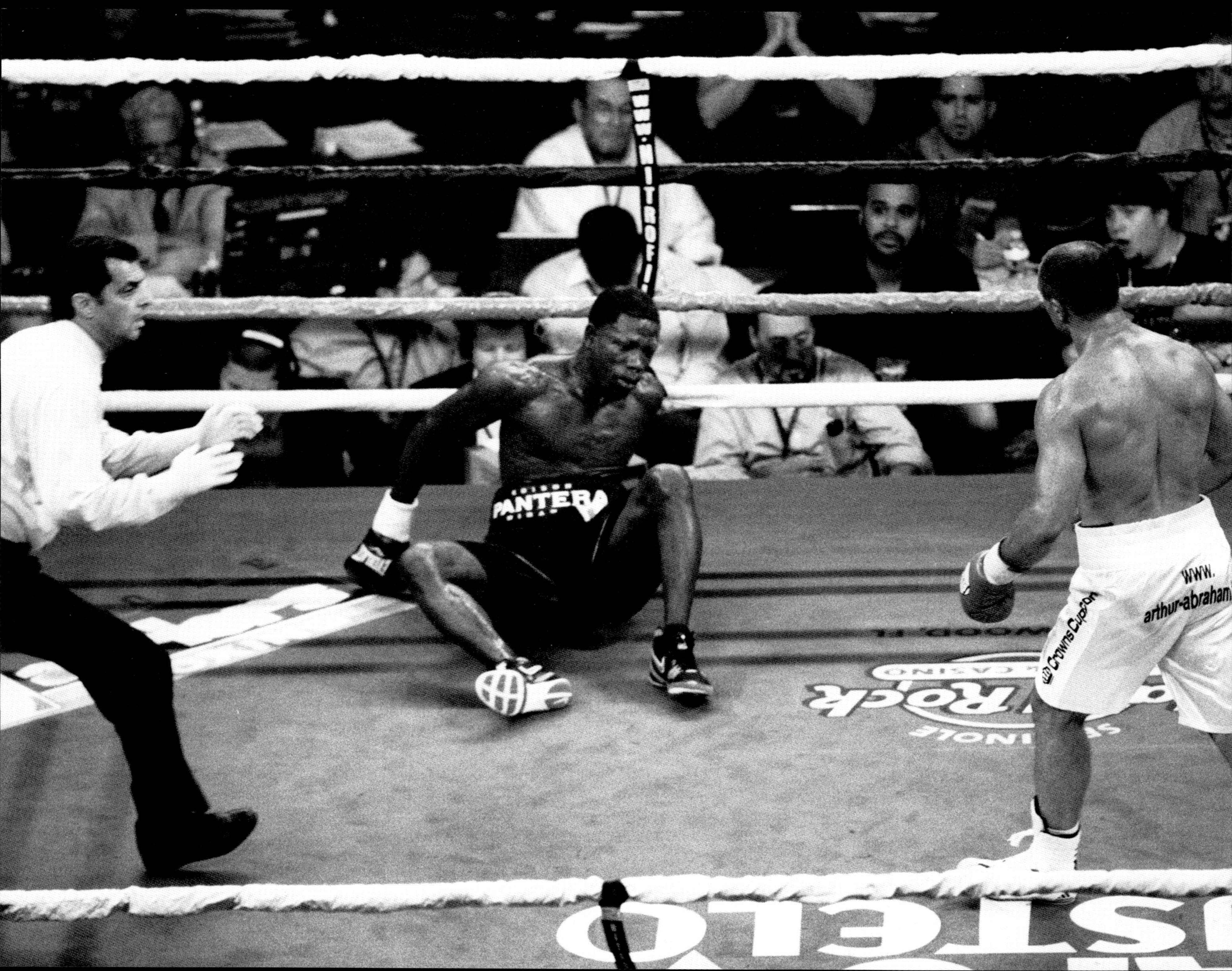
PANTERA
www.
arthur-abraham

Arthur Abraham vs Raúl Márquez
IBF middleweight title
08.11.2008 Jako-Arena
Bamberg, Deutschland
Fotos: Werner Dittmair

Dieser Kampf war der sechste K.o. Sieg in Folge und Márquez überraschte Arthur Abraham durch seine Aufgabe in der 6. Runde. Trotz zwei gebrochener Rippen durch Körpertreffer von dem Amerikaner mit mexikanischer Herkunft in der ersten Runde, wurde Márquez permanent ausgeboxt und hatte niemals die Möglichkeit einer Chance geschweige denn eines Sieges.

This was the sixth K.O victory in a row and Márquez surprised Arthur Abraham by giving up in the sixth round. Despite receiving two broken ribs due to body blows from the American with a Mexican background in the first round, Márquez was permanently outboxed and never had even the hint of a chance of victory.

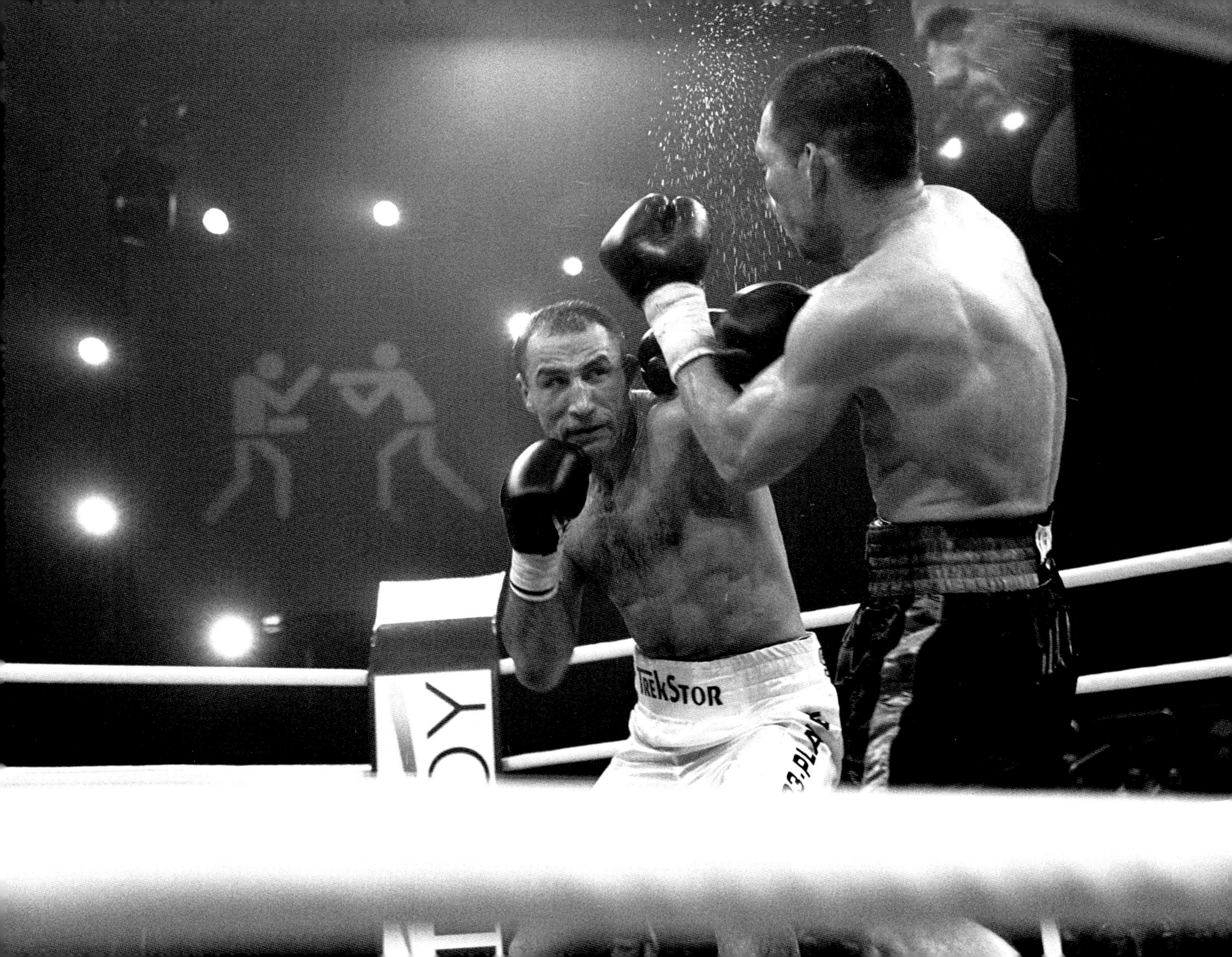
TREKSTOR

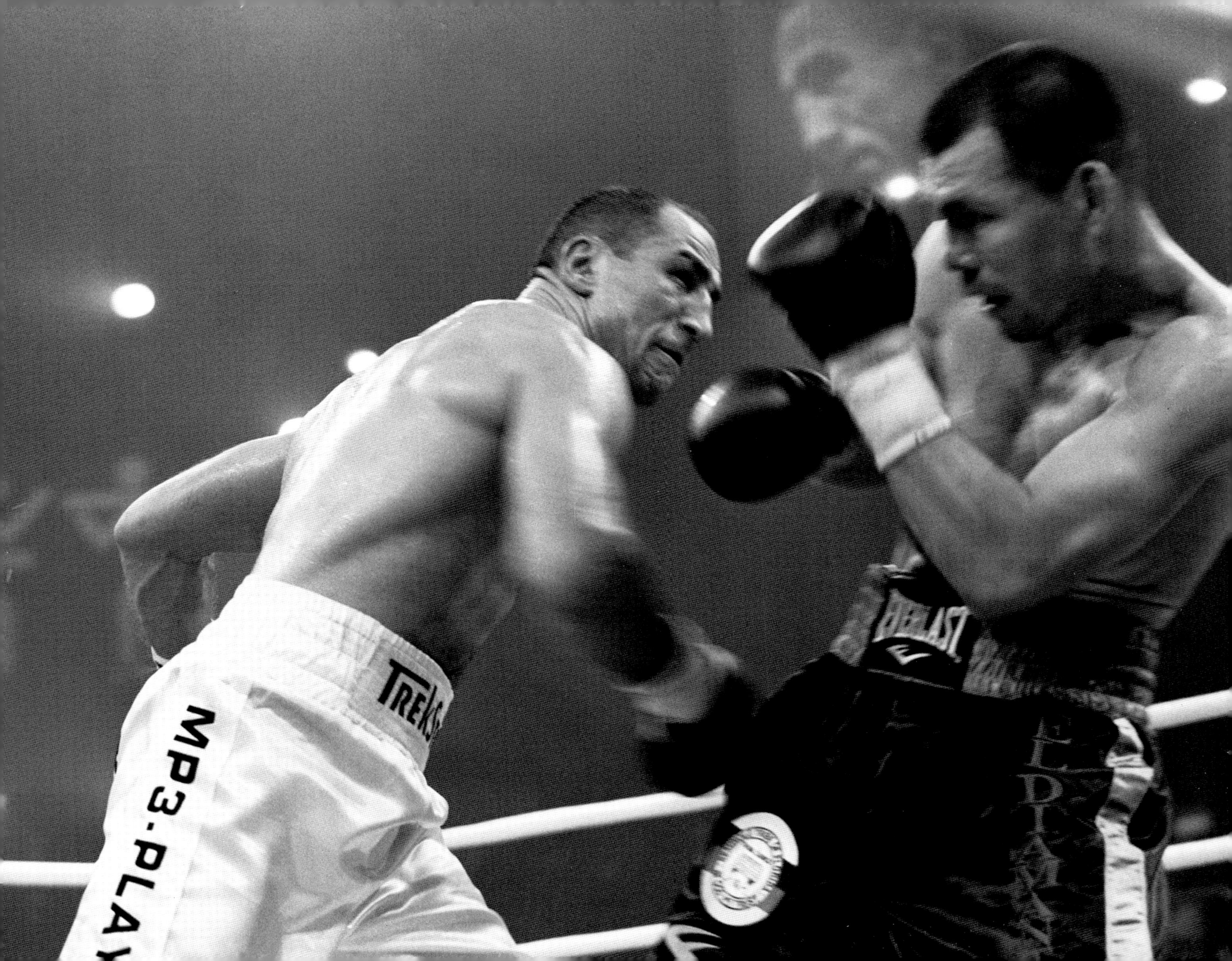
MP3-PLA
EVERLAST

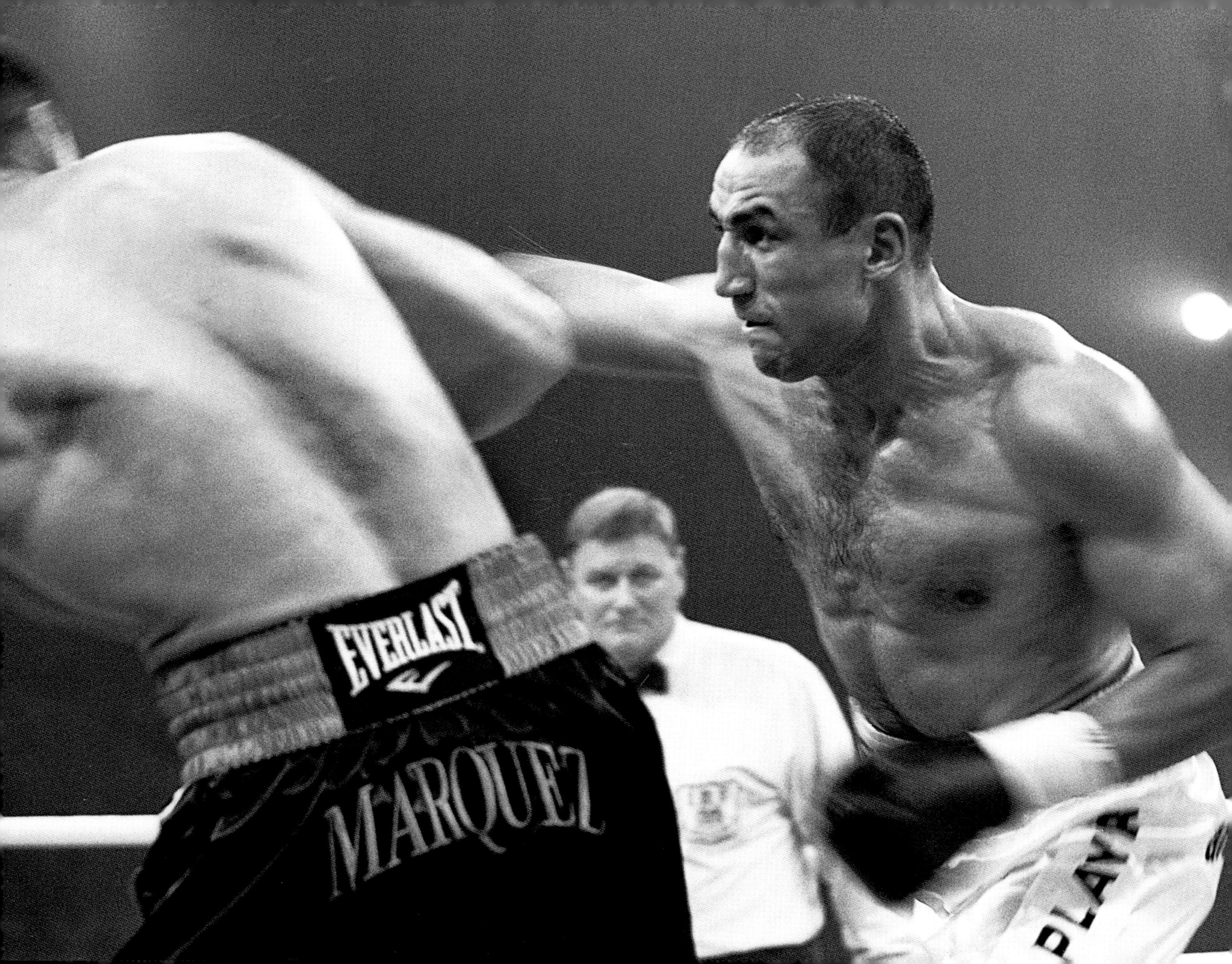
EVERLAST
MARQUEZ
PLAYA

www.Boxfights.com

Arthur und Bruder Alexander

Arthur Abraham vs Lajuan Simon
IBF middleweight title
14.03.2009 Ostseehalle
Kiel, Deutschland
Fotos: Werner Dittmair

Auch in der neunten Titelverteidigung ging King Arthur als einstimmiger Punktsieger hervor. In der gewohnten Art lies er den Amerikaner in den ersten Runden sich wirkungslos an seiner Deckung austoben. In der vierten Runde überraschte der Amerikaner mit sehr starken Nehmerqualitäten. Die siebte Runde sollte eine Entscheidung herbeiführen aber Simon konnte sich dem finalen K.o. Schlag geschickt entziehen. Kurzzeitige Schwächeerscheinungen in der 8. Runde, hervorgerufen durch seine vorherige Powerrunde, hat der King jedoch clever bewältigt.

King Arthur won again with a unanimous points' decision in his ninth title defence. In his usual style, he let the American test his defences without any impact in the first round. In the fourth round, the American surprisingly showed an exceptional resistance. The seventh round should have delivered the ultimate K.O, but Simon skilfully avoided the telling blow. In the eighth round, the King cleverly overcame brief signs of weakness, brought on by his exertions in the previous round.

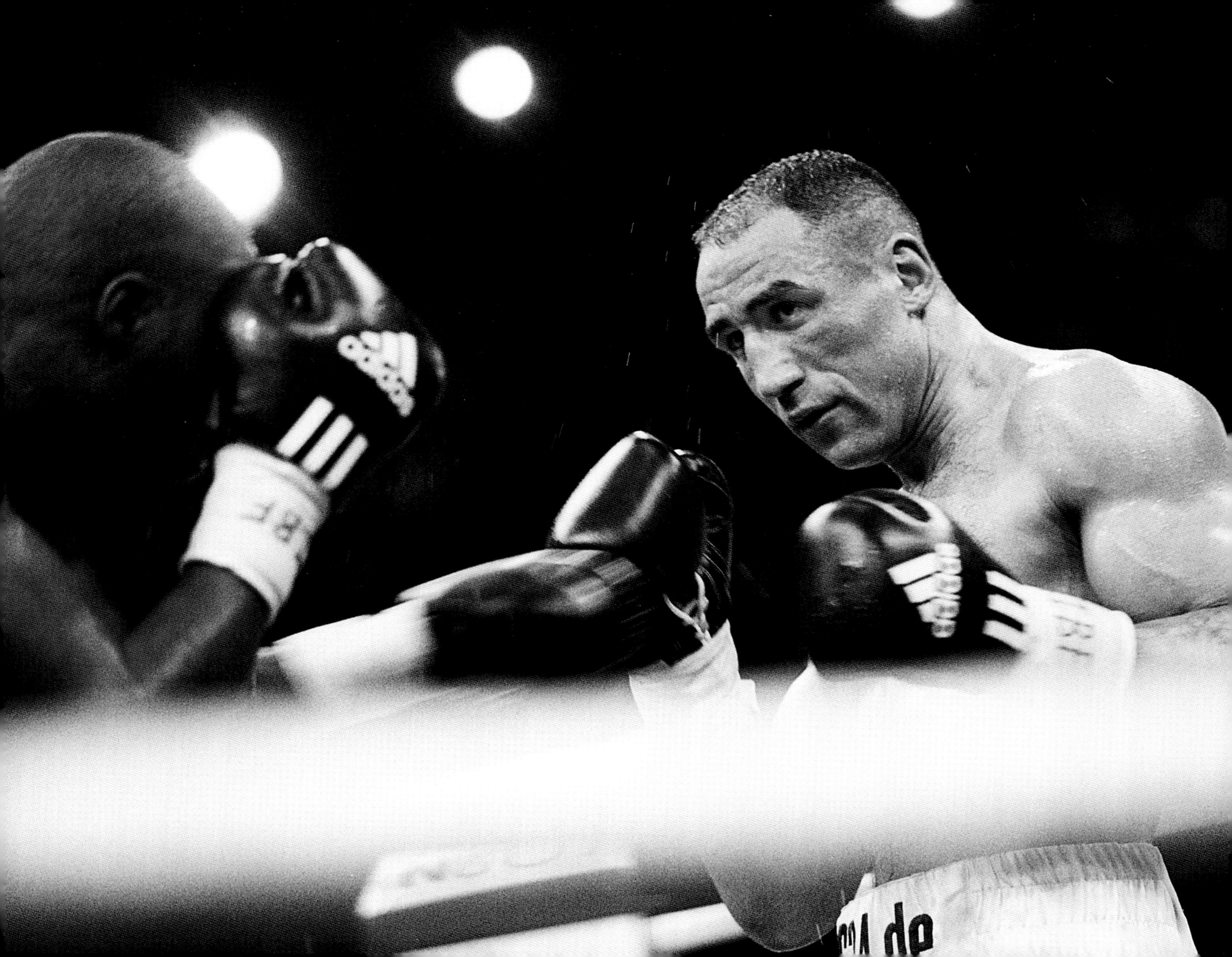

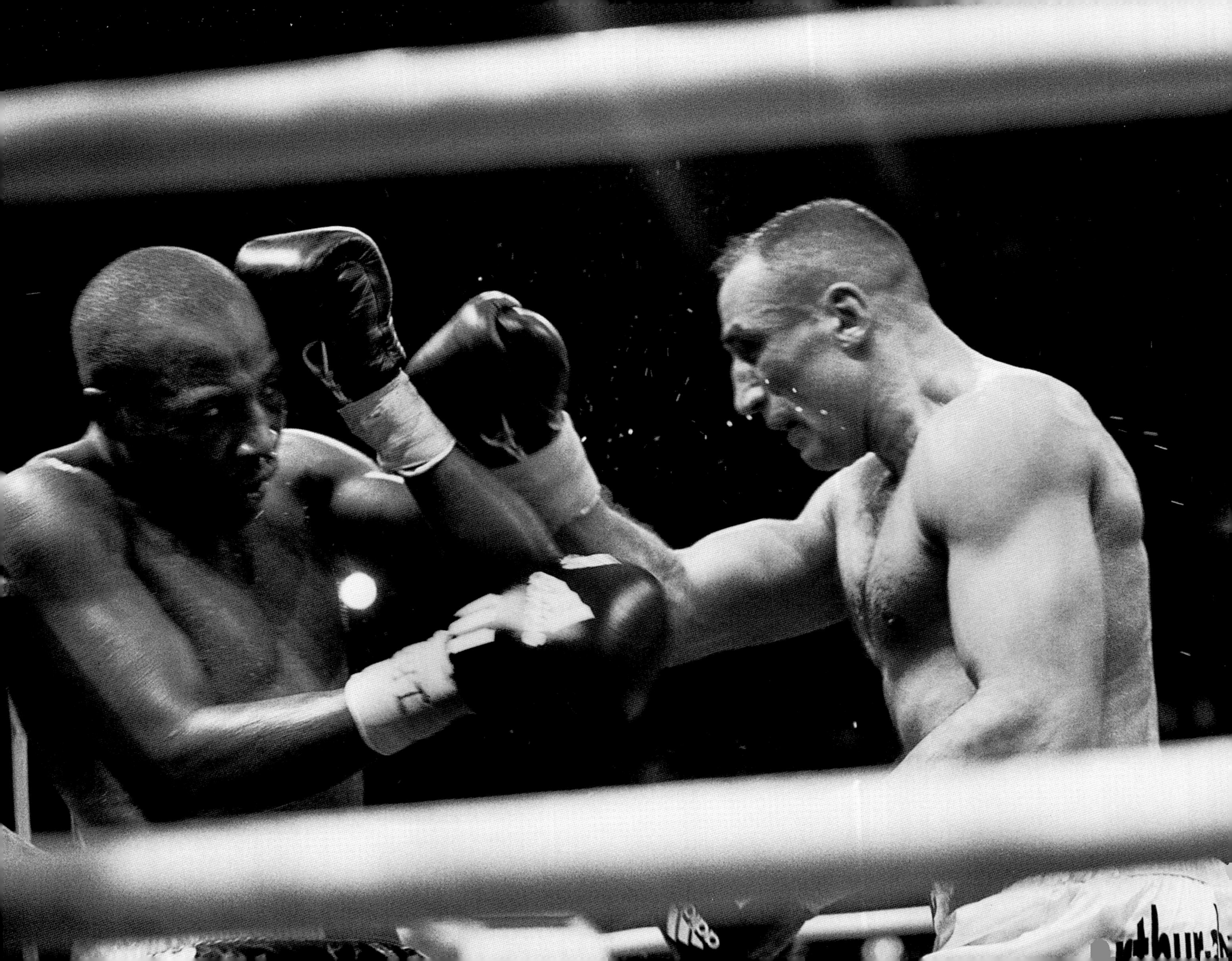

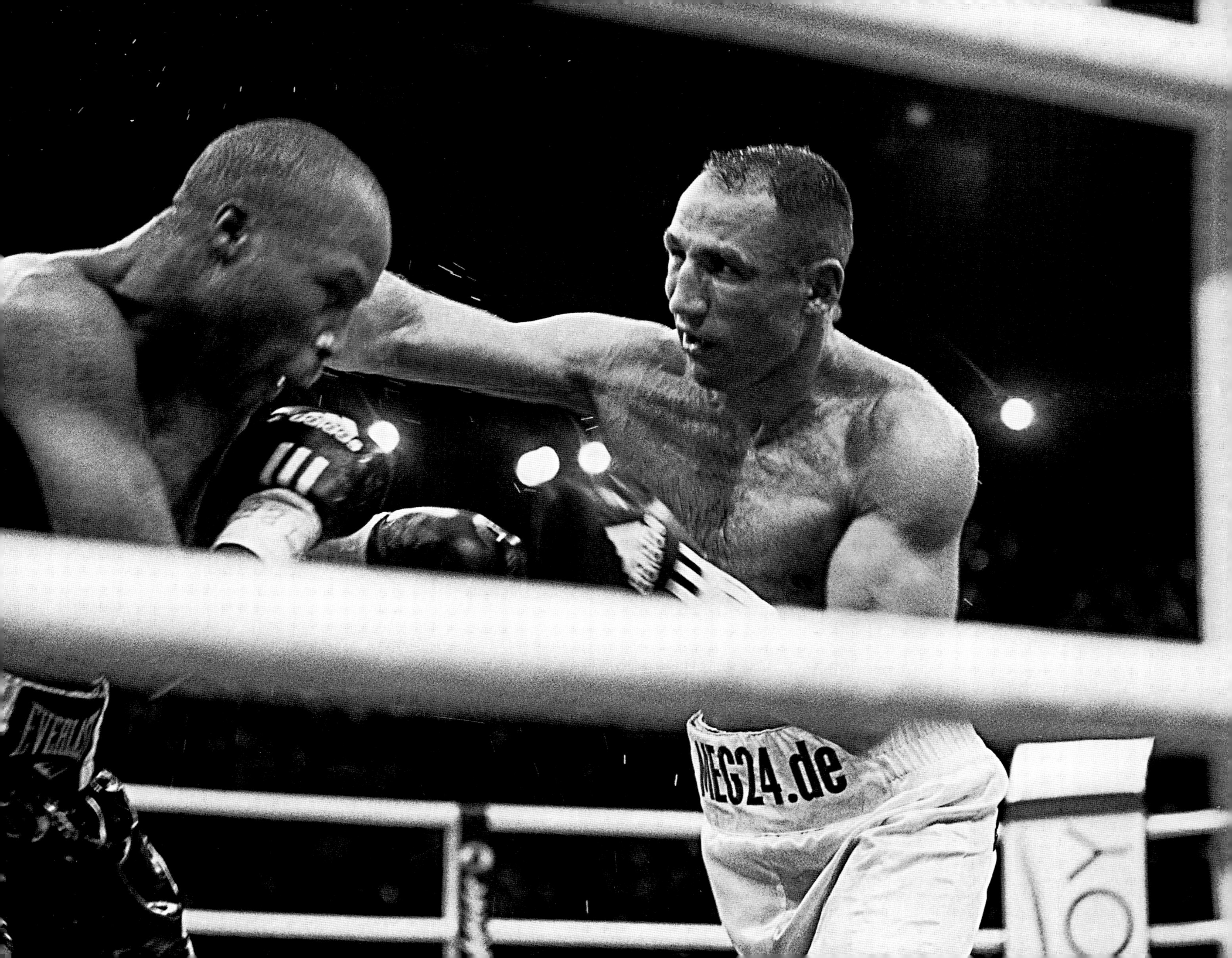
MEG24.de

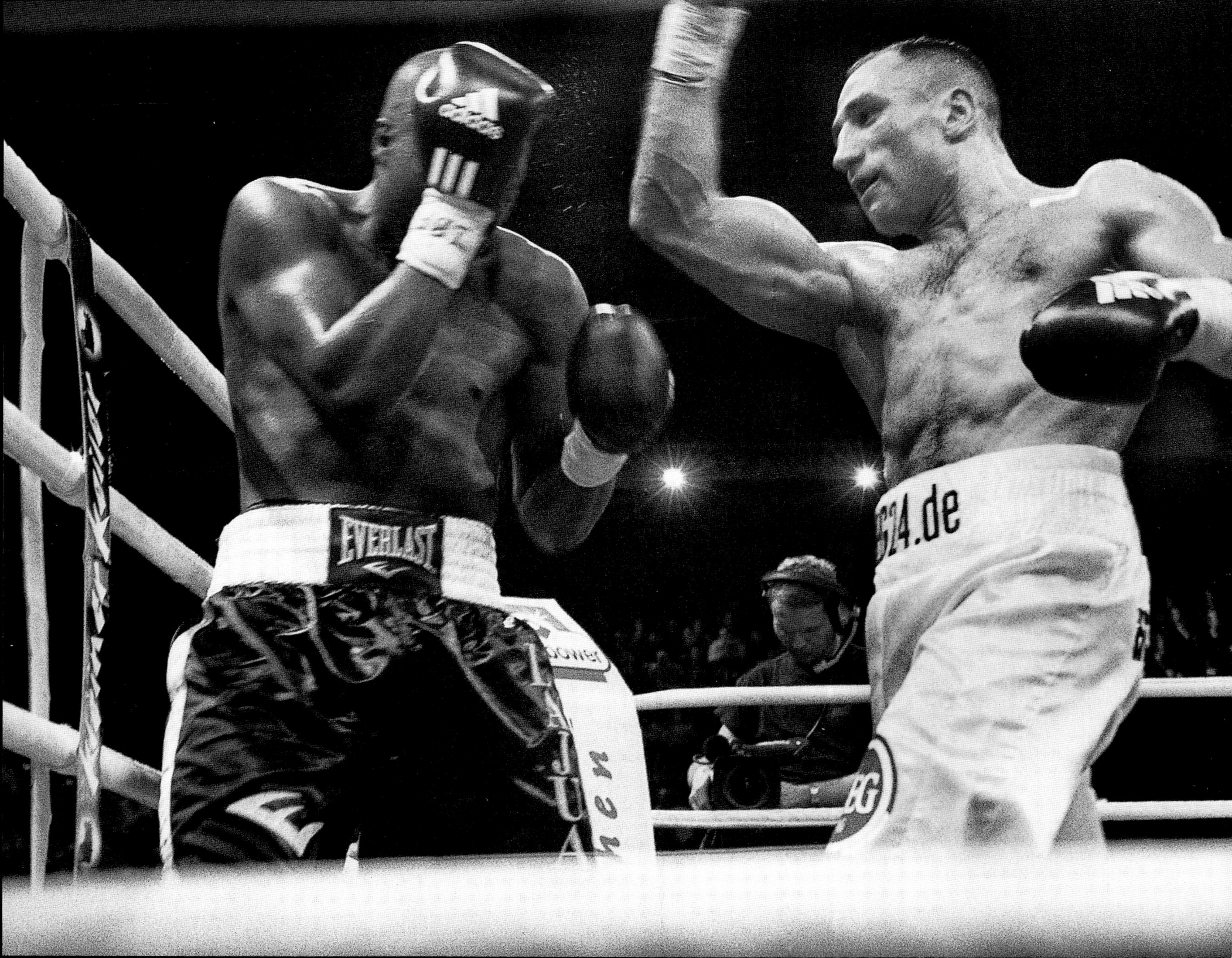
EVERLAST

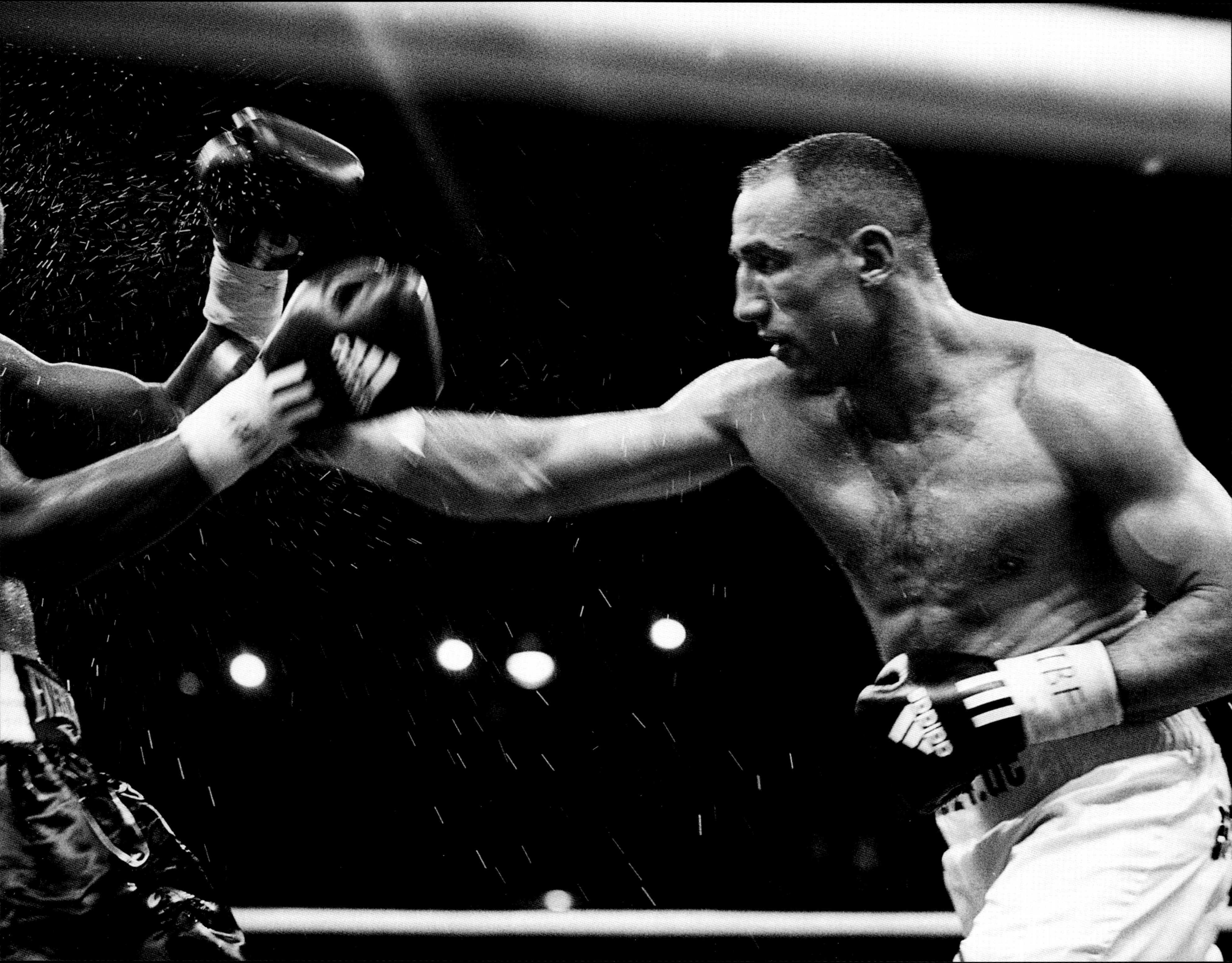

Arthur Abraham vs Mahir Oral
IBF middleweight title
27.06.2009 Max Schmeling Halle
Berlin, Deutschland
Fotos: Werner Dittmair

Auch in seinem letzten Mittelgewichtskampf siegt Arthur Abraham durch TKO über den beherzten und sympathischen ARENA Boxer Mahir Oral. In der 10. Runde warf Orals Trainer das Handtuch. Während der ersten 3 Runden forderte der aktivere ORAL den Titelverteidiger immer wieder. Der Spätstarter Arthur Abraham verbuchte ab der 4. Runde mit mehreren Niederschlägen des Gegners reichlich Punkte für sich.

Arthur Abraham also won his final Middleweight fight through a technical knockout against the courageous and likable ARENA boxer Mahir Oral. In the 10th round, Oral's trainer threw in the towel. The more active ORAL tested the title holder continuously throughout the first three rounds. Arthur Abraham, famed for his late starts, then picked up point after point from the fourth round for the numerous blows that he landed.

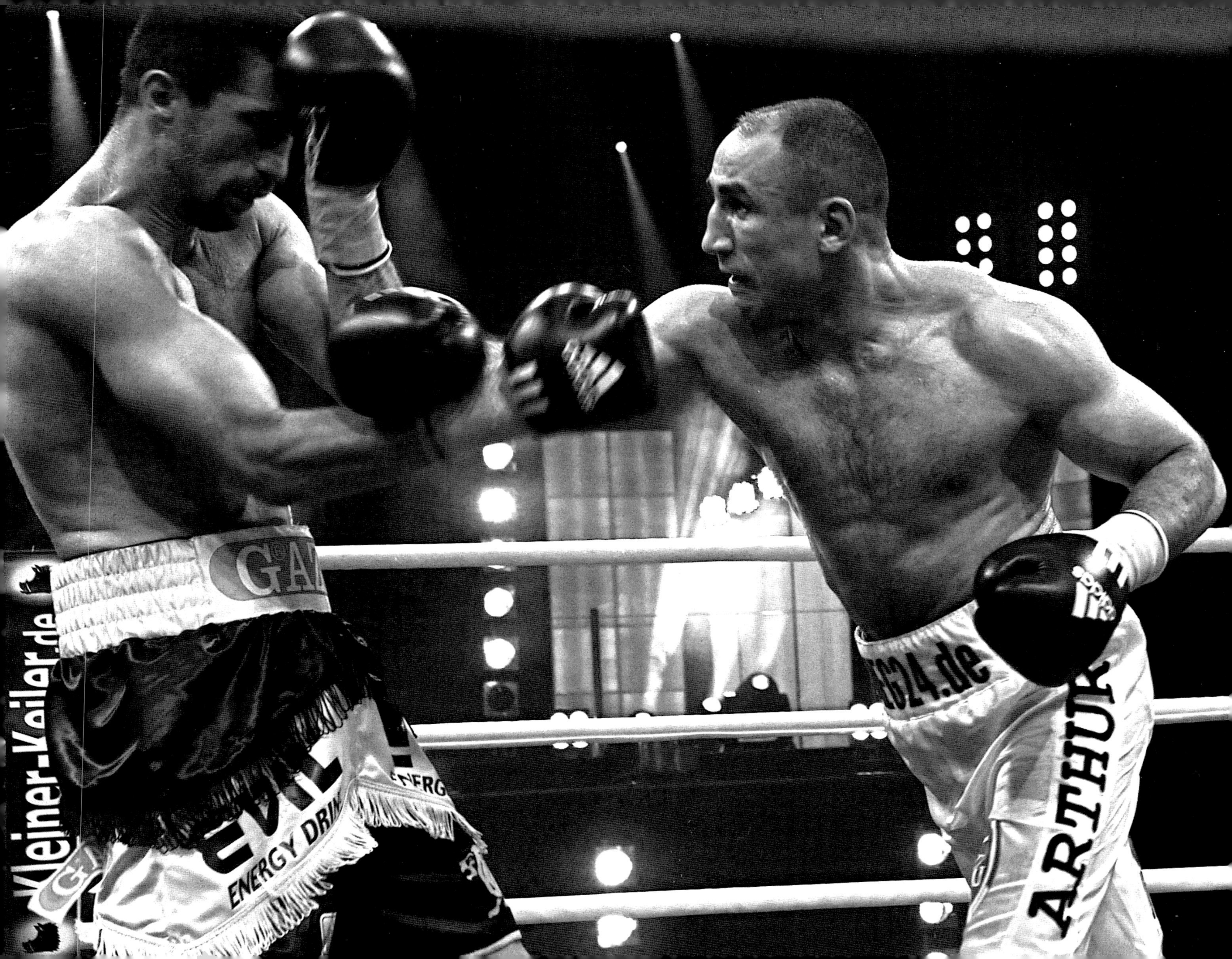
ARTHUR

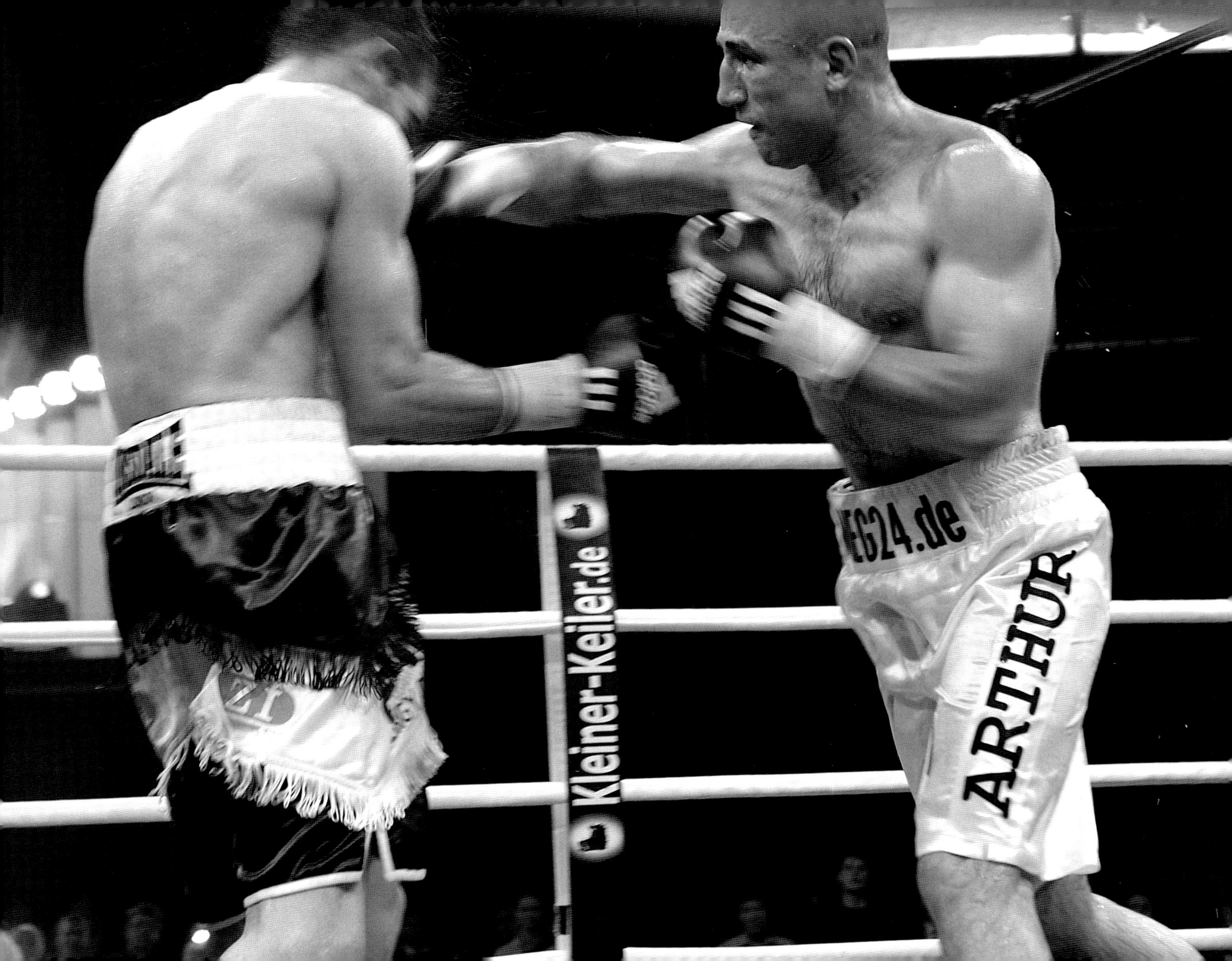
Kleiner-Keiler.de
EG24.de
ARTHUR

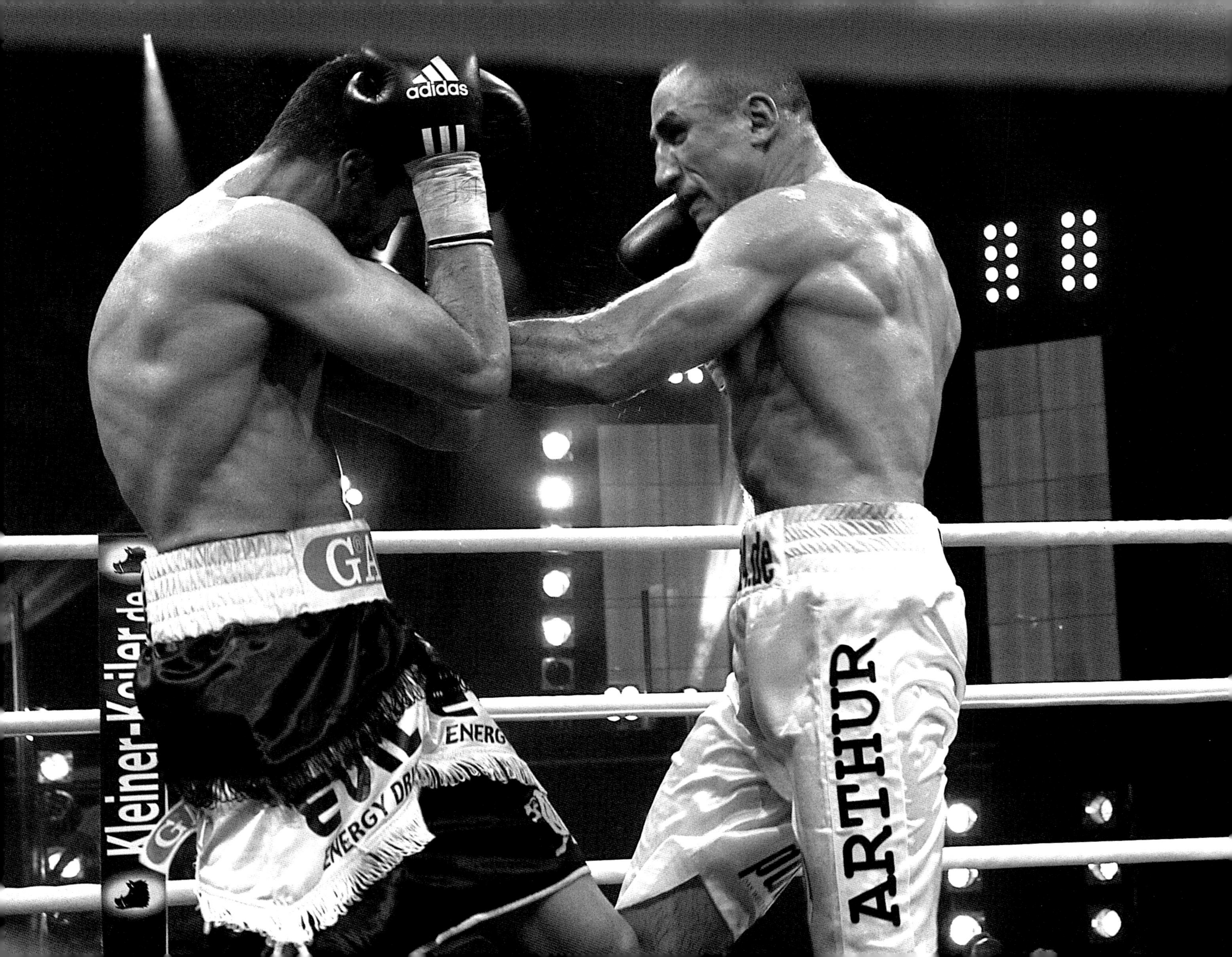
adidas
ARTHUR

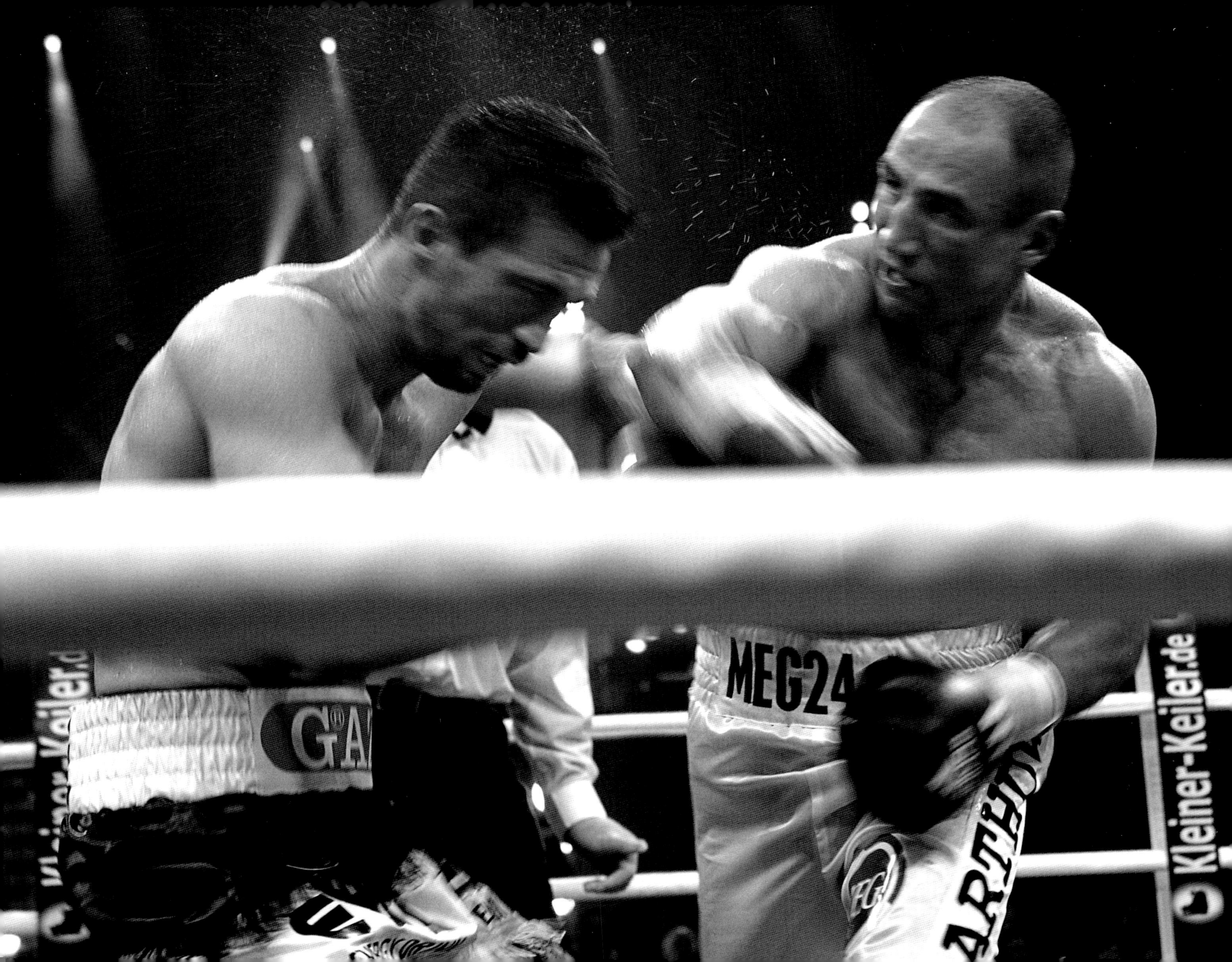
MEG24
Kleiner-Keiler.de

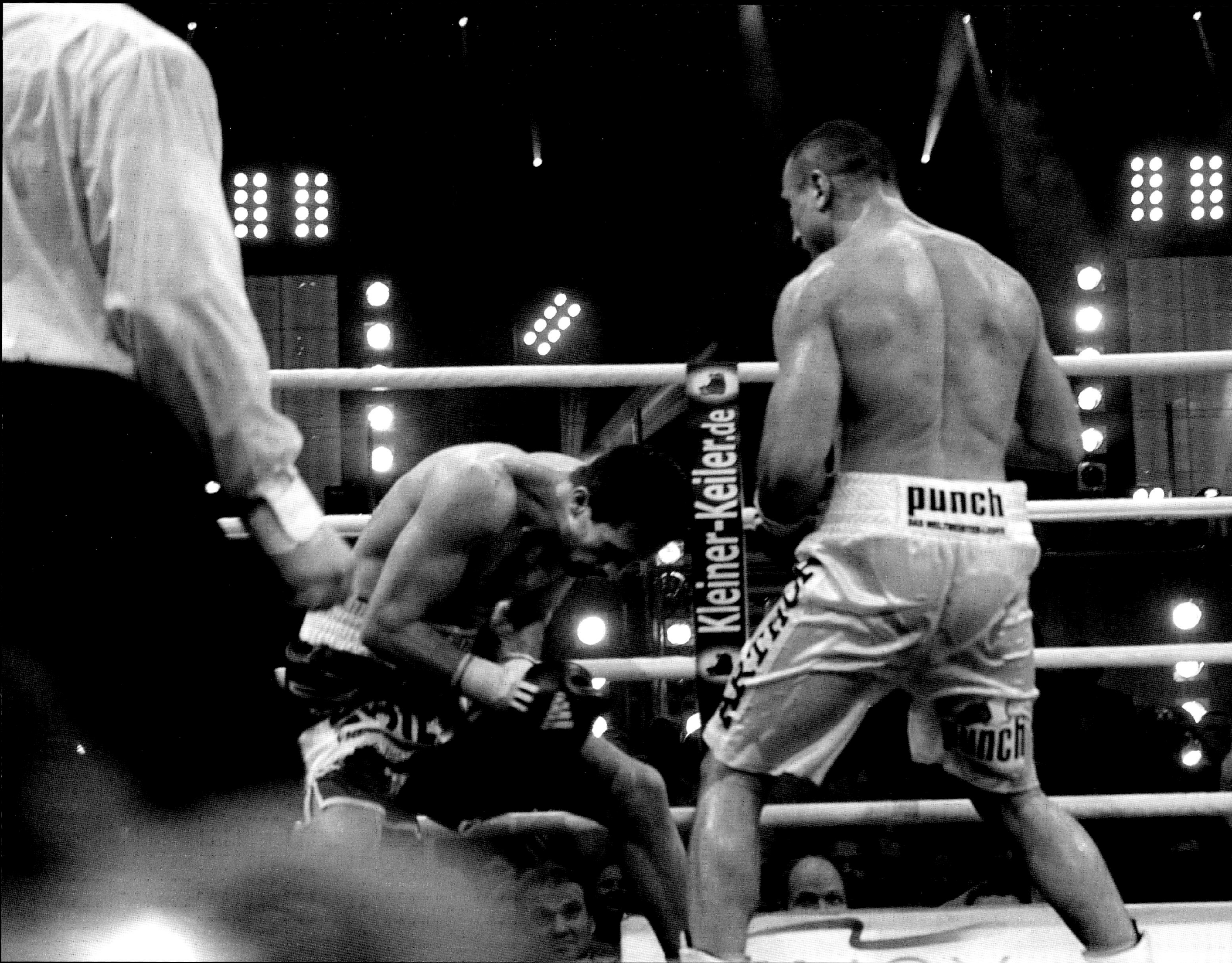
Kleiner-Keiler.de
punch

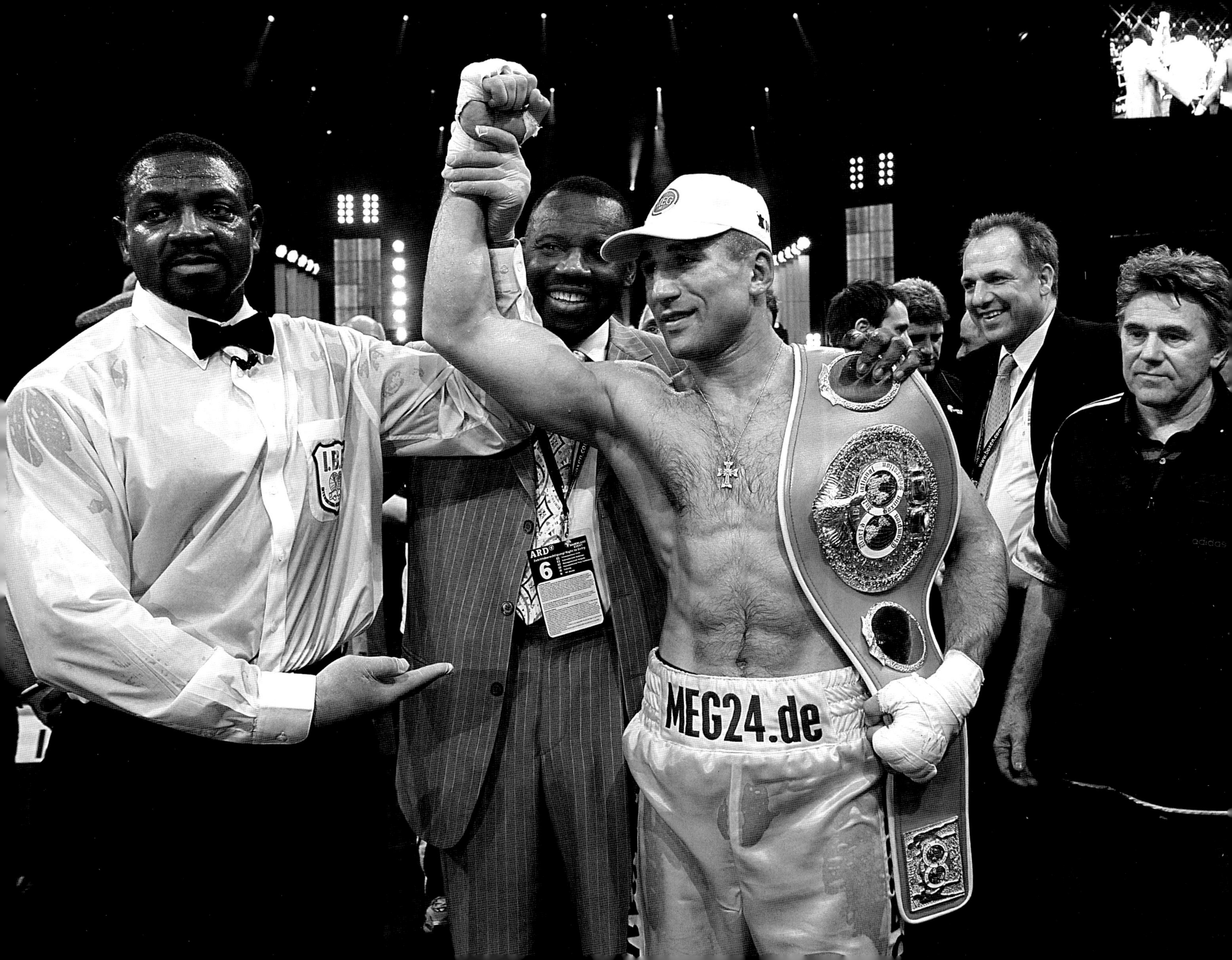
MEG24.de
ARD
6

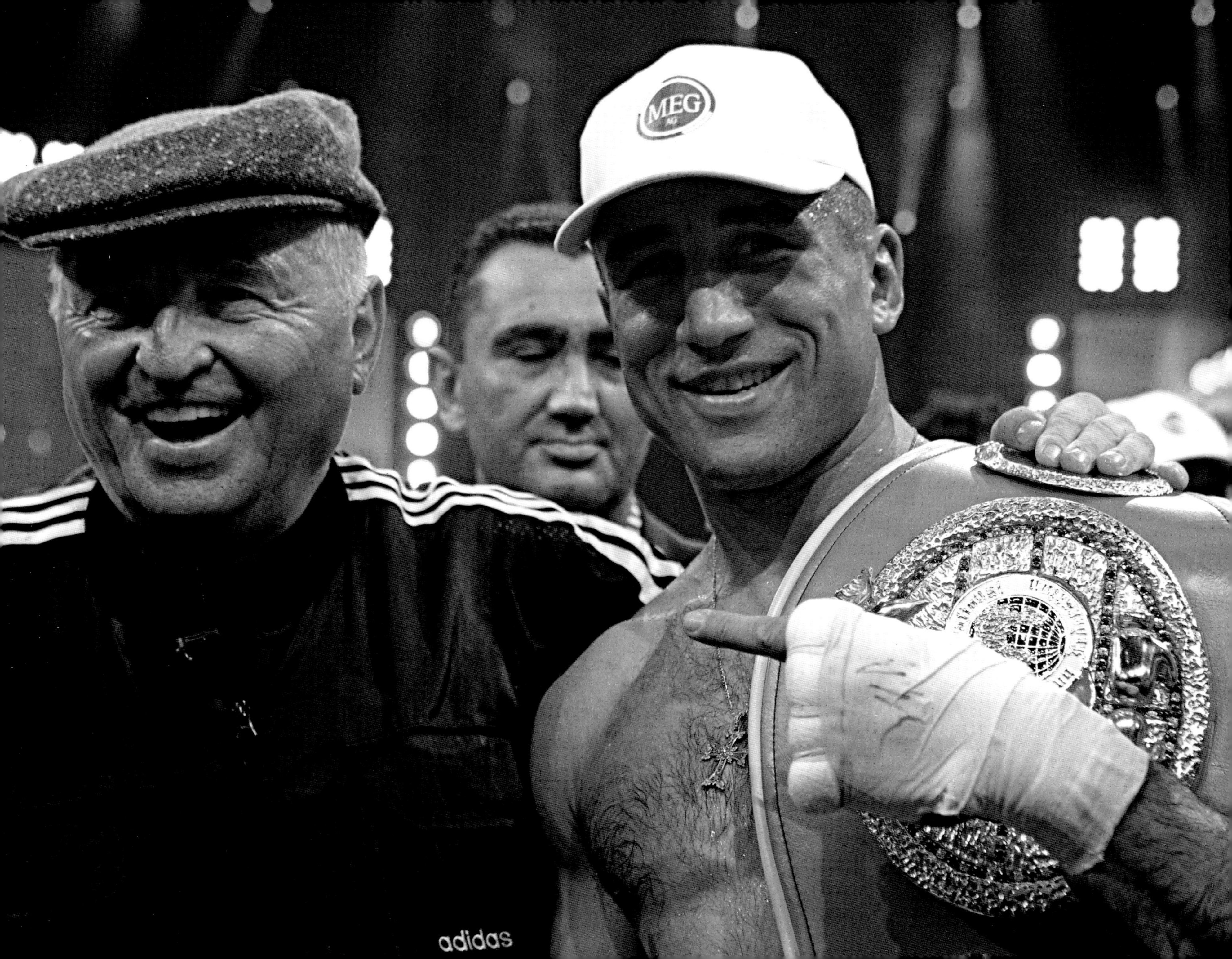
MEG
adidas

**Trainingslager
Zinnowitz/Usedom
Bundesleistungszentrum Kienbaum/Berlin**

Zinnowitz/Usedom

Zinnowitz/Usedom

Kienbaum/Berlin

Kienbaum/Berlin

Kienbaum/Berlin

ES GEHT UM ALLES

Ein Film von Nina Pourlak und Sebastian Lempe. Ein facettenreicher und authentischer Dokumentarfilm über die Beziehung zwischen Trainer und Boxer. Ulli Wegner als Vaterfigur, Trainer & Lehrer. Prädikat für den Arthur & Ulli Fan: SEHENSWERT.

A multifaceted and authentic documenatary about the relationship between the trainer and his boxer. Ulli Wegner is the father figure, the trainer and the teacher. Not to be missed for all fans of Arthur & Ulli!

ES GEHT UM ALLES

Ulli Wegner, Nina Pourlak, Arthur Abraham und Sebastian Lempe bei der Film-Premiere in Berlin

Arthur und Bruder Alexander Abraham

Familie Abraham

Arthur´s 29. Geburtstagsparty in Ritz-Carlton, Berlin

MAX SCHMELING

ein Film von Uwe Boll
im Verleih der Central Film Berlin und KSM München

Arthur Abraham spielt die Rolle des Richard (Riedl) Vogt, welcher der letzte Gegner vom Max Schmeling war. Max Schmeling verlor am 31.10.1948 in der Berliner Waldbühne in der 10. und letzten Runde nach Punkten und gab direkt danach seinen Rücktritt vom Boxsport bekannt.

Arthur Abraham played the role of Richard (Riedl) Vogt, who was the last opponent of Max Schmeling. Max Schmeling lost on October 31, 1948, in the Berliner Waldbühne in the 10th and last round on a points' decision and he immediately announced his retirement from boxing.

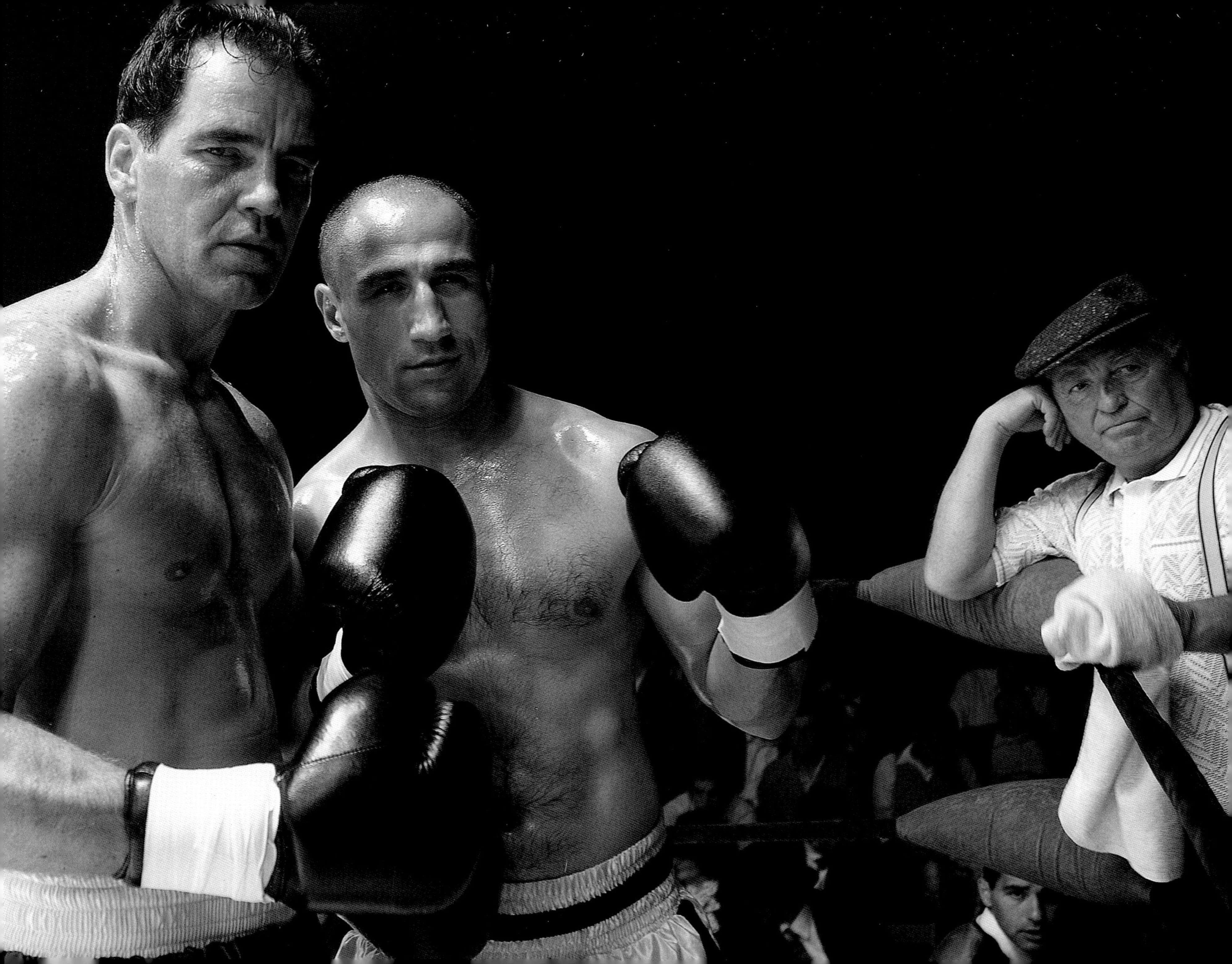

Arthur Abraham (Riedl Vogt) und Henry Maske (Max Schmeling) beim Dreh in Zagreb

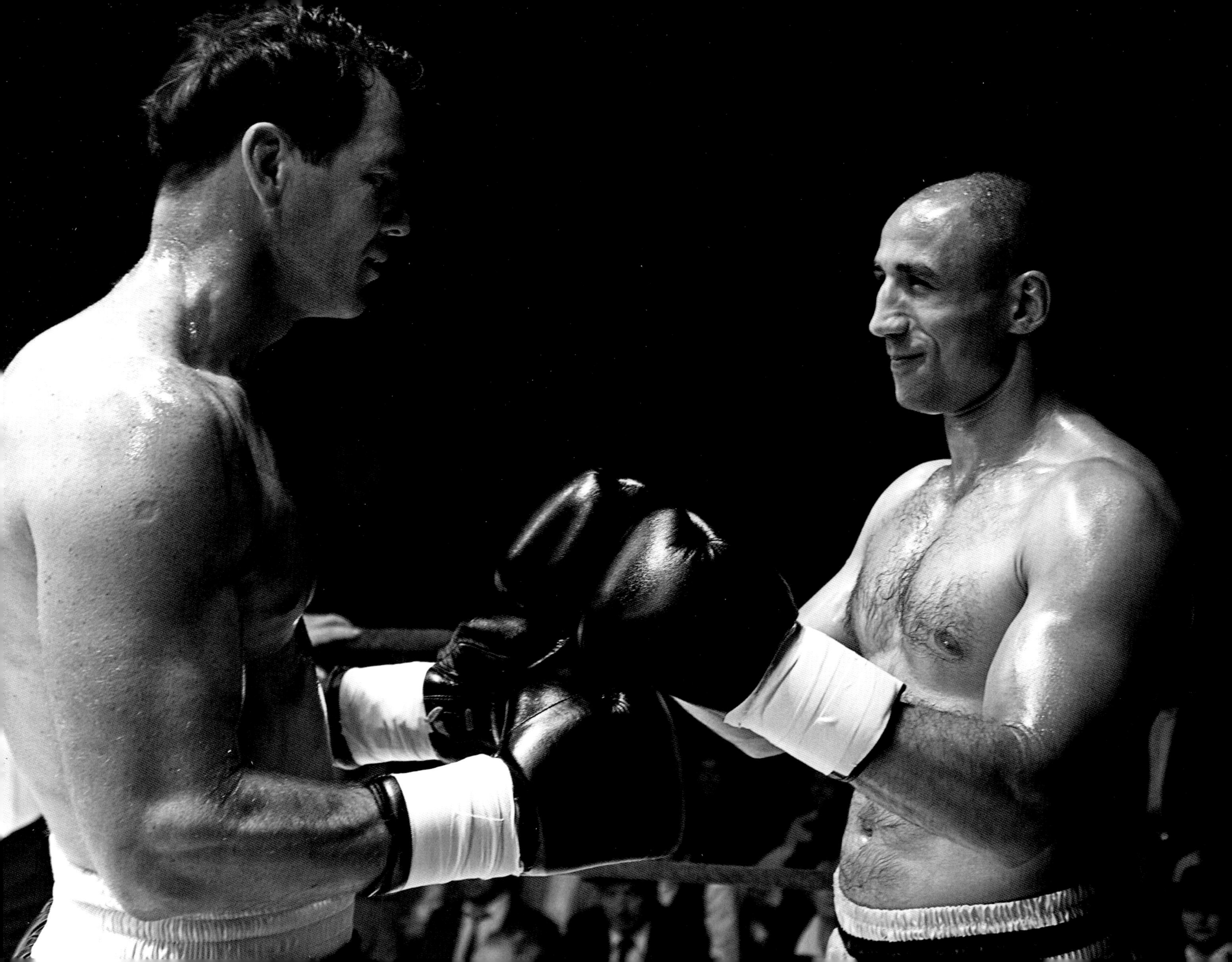

Arthur Abraham, Henry Maske und Heino Ferch

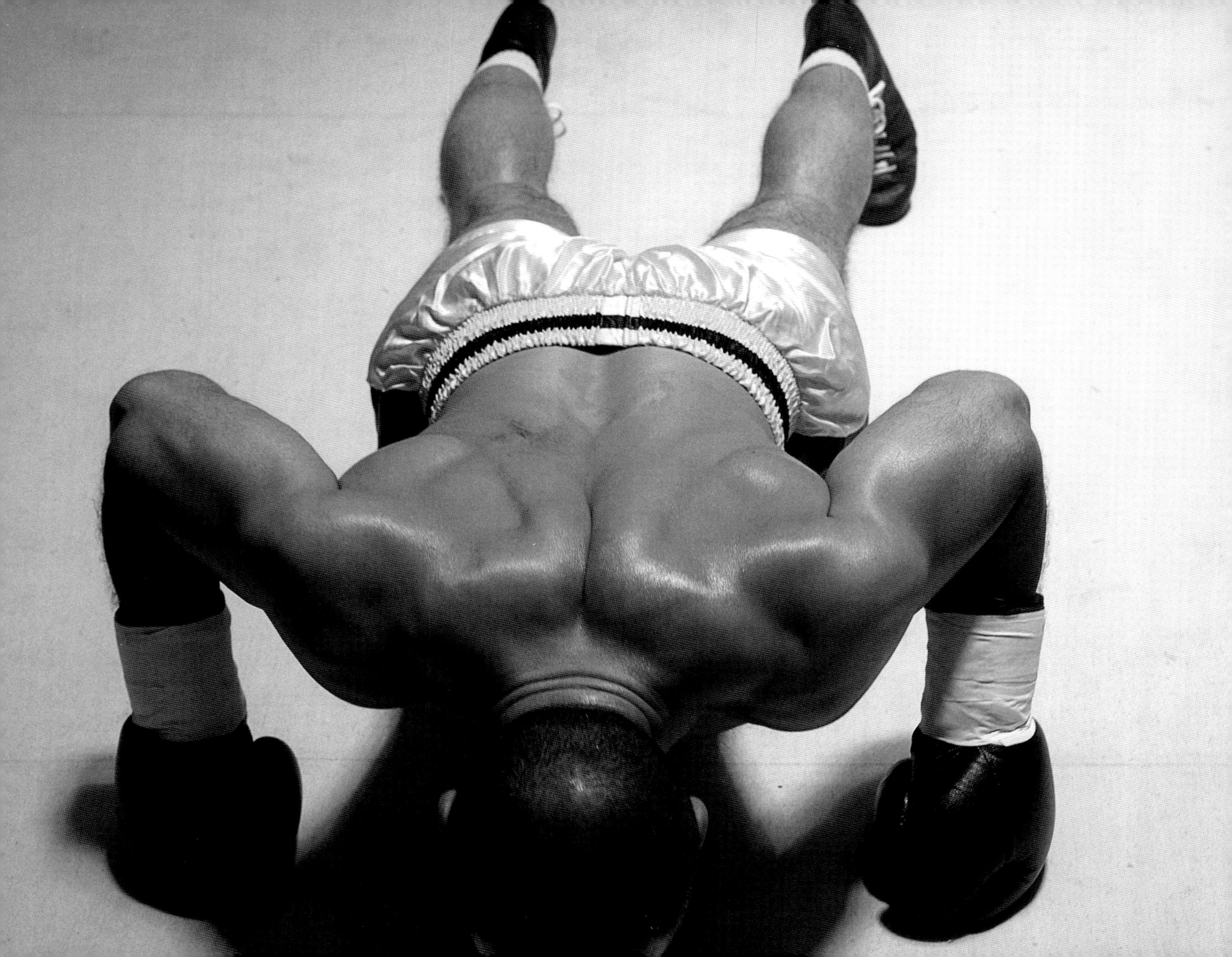

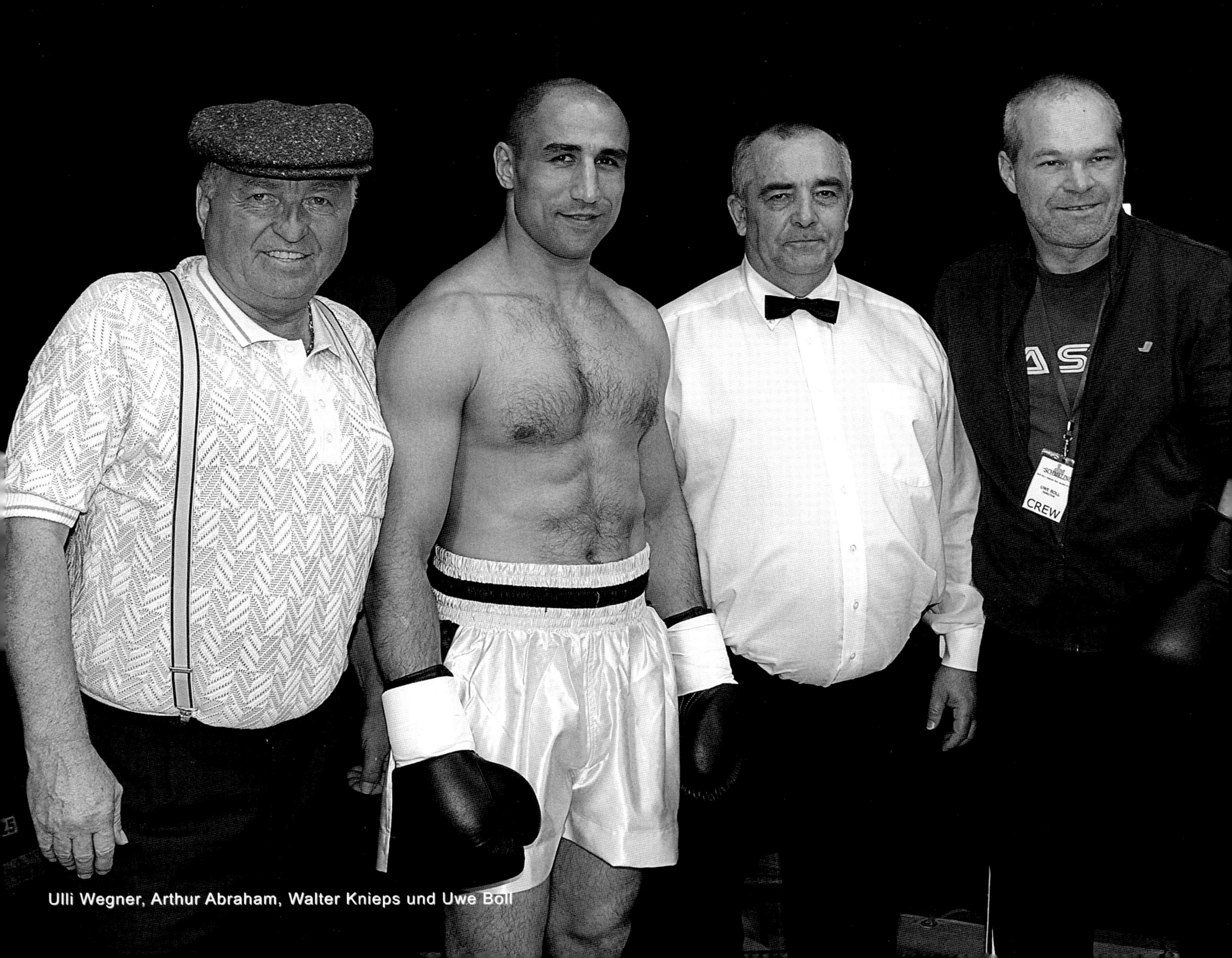

Ulli Wegner, Arthur Abraham, Walter Knieps und Uwe Boll

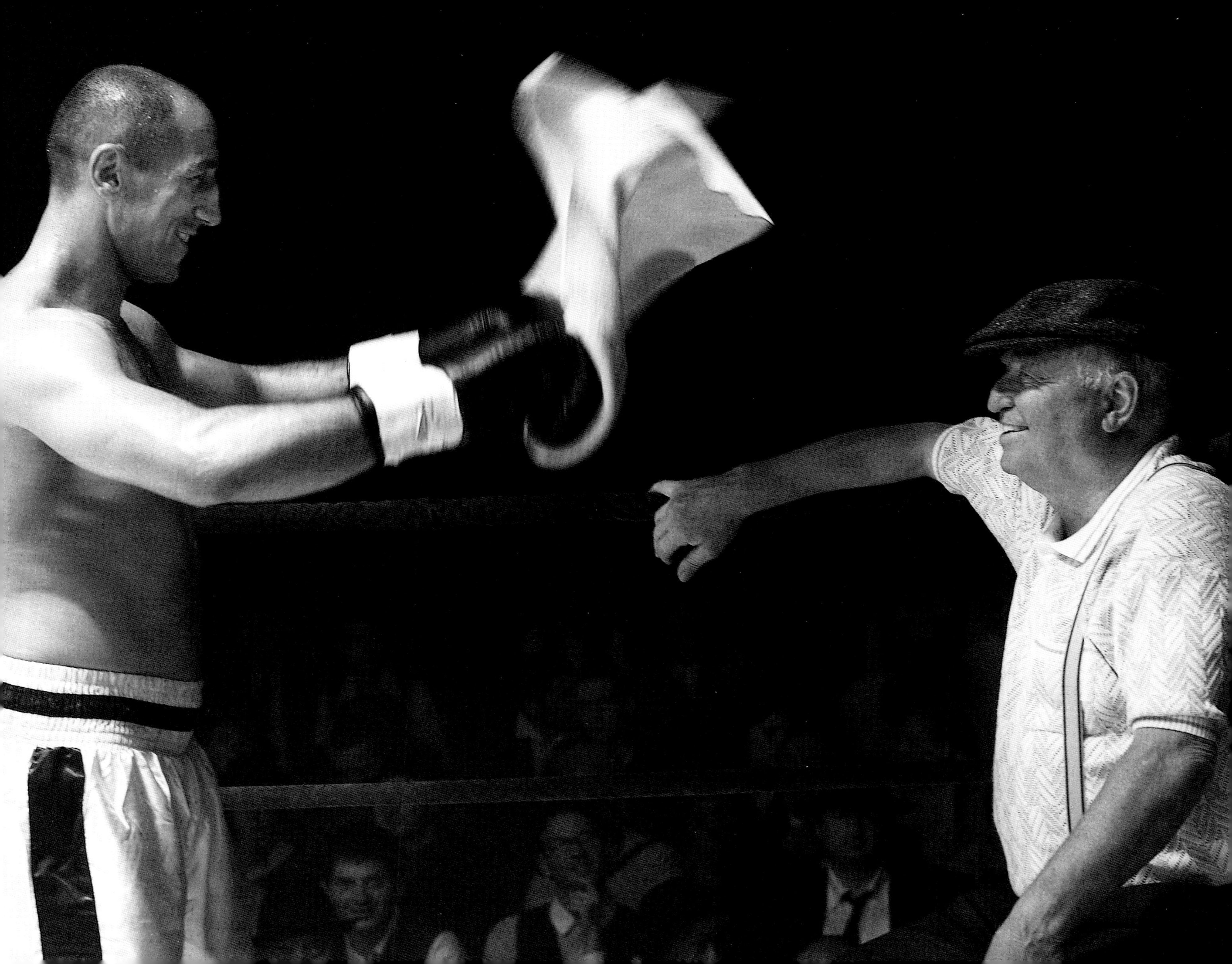

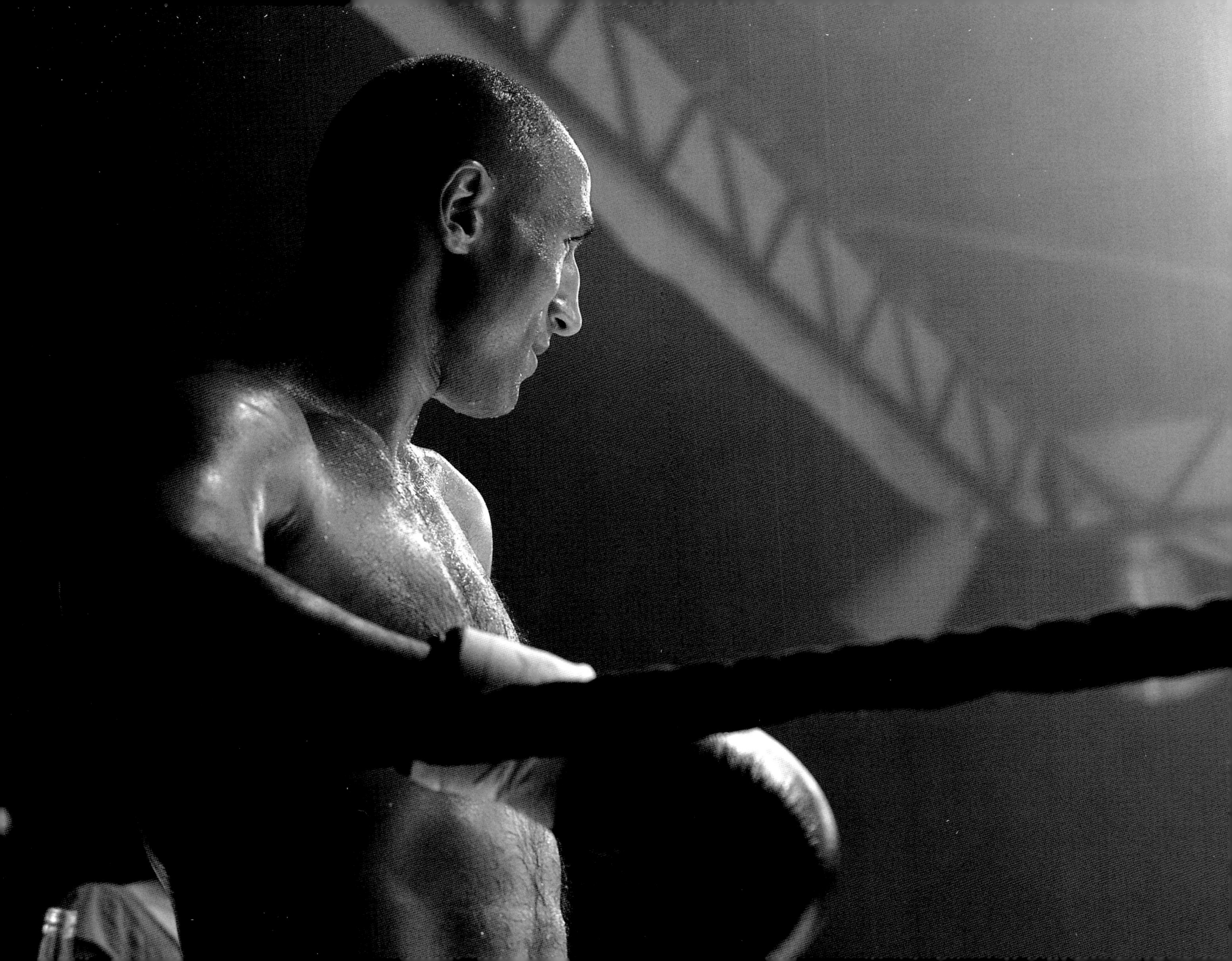

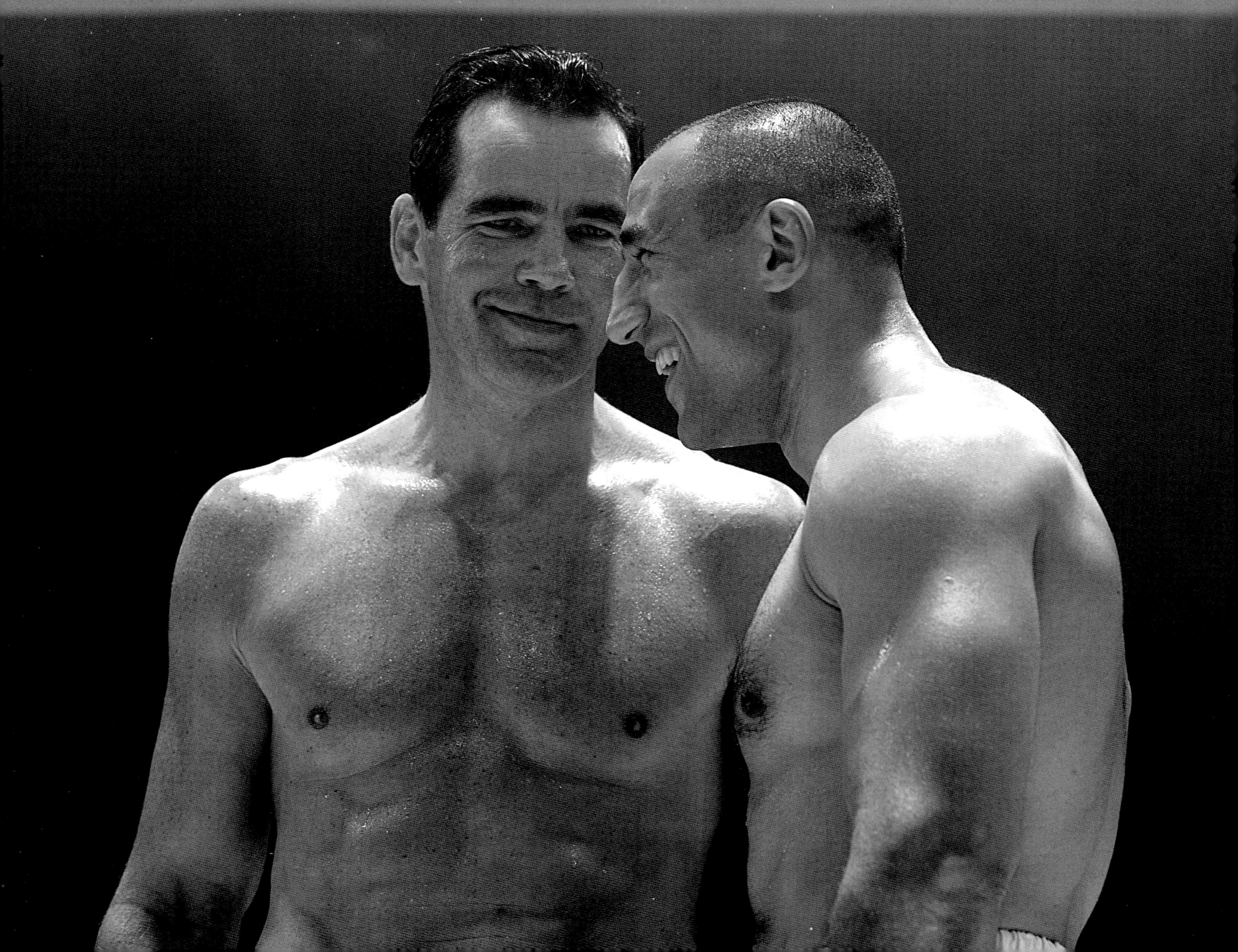

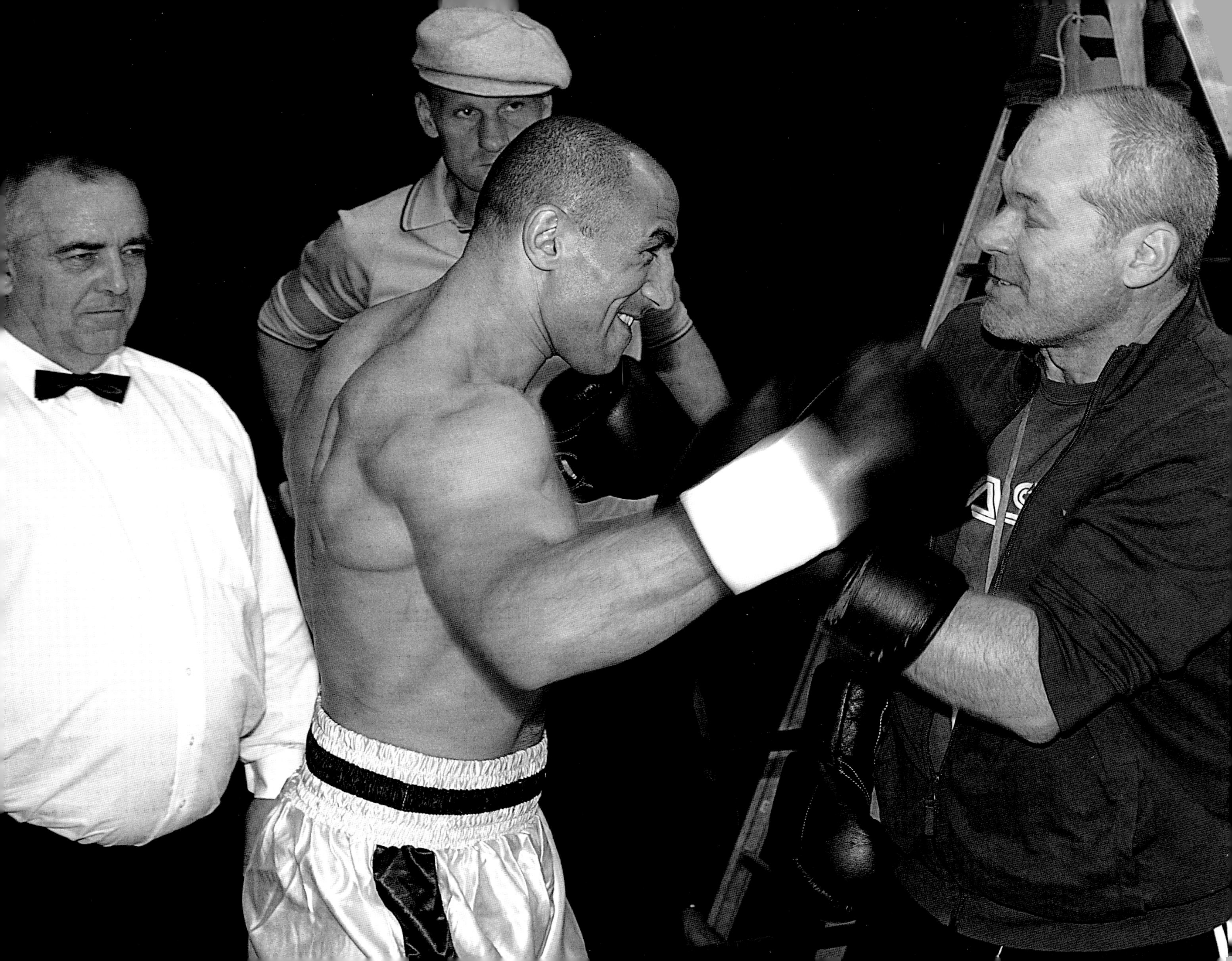

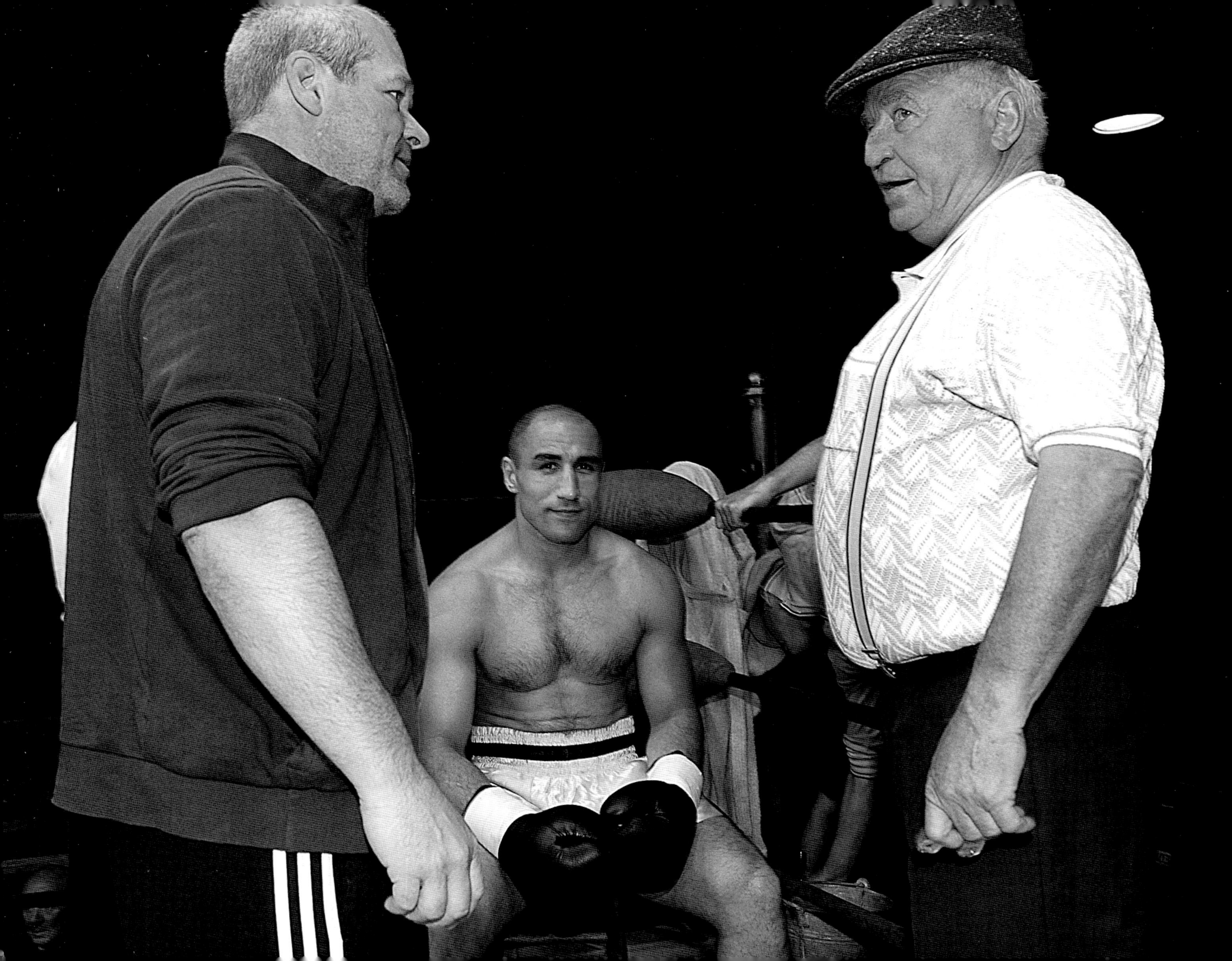

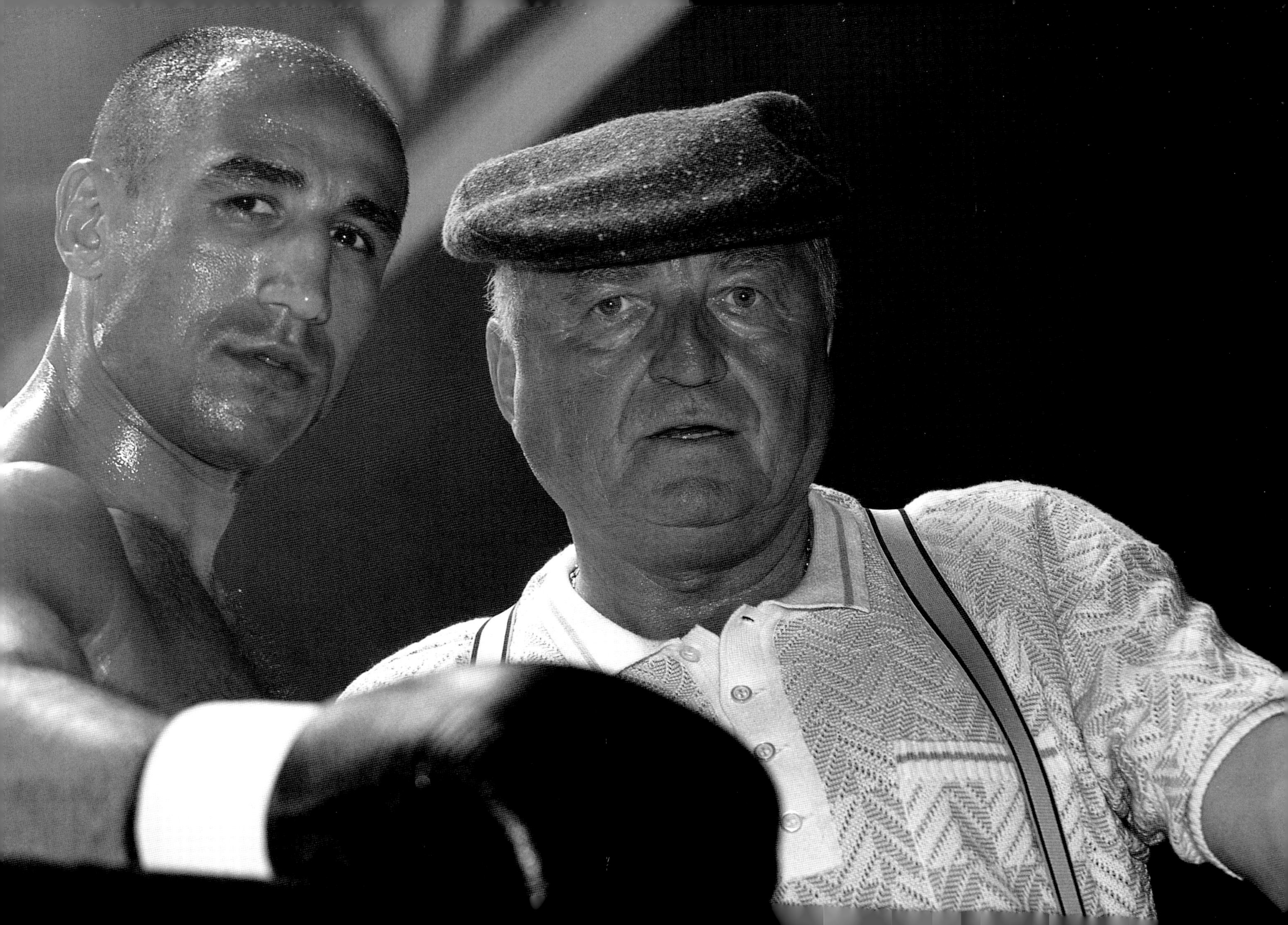

www.Starplanet-Verlag.de

Impressum

Das Werk ist einschließlich all seiner Teile urheberrechtlich geschützt. Jede Verwertung, insbesondere Vervielfältigungen, Übersetzungen, Mikroverfilmungen und die Einspeicherung und Verarbeitung in elektronischen Systemen ist nur mit schriftlichen Genehmigung und Quellenangabe gestattet.

Fotos
Marianne Müller & Werner Dittmair

Text
Werner Dittmair

Layout & Bildbearbeitung
Gustavo Prado

English version
Benjamin Peter Gladwell

Starplanet Verlag und Bildagentur
Barbarossastr. 2
60388 Frankfurt

Tel. +49 177 60 85 400
Fax +49 6109 369 703

e-Mail info@starplanet.de

2011 © Starplanet-Verlag

Starplanet-Verlag

ABRAHAM BOXSPORT GMBH

CAMP DAVID **Boxfights.com** **Walter Staudinger**

SAUERLAND EVENT

Cyberpartner GmbH